Drawing on decades of experience in preaching the Bible, Bob Fyall's compact, but rich, answer to the title question deserves to be read and pondered by everyone who preaches. I particularly appreciated its blended emphases on the practical pastoral theology which should animate the preacher, along with the need to be totally dependent on the work of the Holy Spirit to regain the supernatural in our preaching.

Realistic and down to earth this book is full of Biblical insights and unswerving confidence in the whole sweep of Scripture. It contains many memorable nuggets of exposition, information, and practical hints, to set the beginner on the right road, to stimulate the weary and jaded, and to stir up every preacher to work hard in order to do the job better. Here is a sure guide to eradicate boredom from the pulpit.

DAVID JACKMAN
Former President, the Proclamation Trust, London.

T0001588

Why
Are We Often
So Boring?
Reflections on Preaching

Bob Fyall

CHRISTIAN
FOCUS

Contents

Foreword

This is a book whose goal is to enrich the worship of the church. Its focus is therefore on the preacher, whose task it is to attune the ears of God's people to hear the voice of Christ Himself, the church's true worship leader, so they will respond in obedient faith, bowing the knee to Him – that is, in true and living worship.

Worship is giving all of oneself to God and *for* God, and only through the Word of the gospel can human beings be restored, and continually renewed, for true worship. According to the Bible therefore, the ear (hearing) not the mouth (singing) has always been the chief organ of corporate worship: 'Guard your steps when you go to the house of God. To draw near to listen is better than to offer the sacrifice of fools...be not rash with your mouth' (Eccles. 5:1-2). 'Faith comes from *hearing*, and hearing through the word of Christ' (Rom. 10:17). God's Word is the only true worship leader in the church, and must be heard. 'And how are they to hear without someone preaching?' (Rom. 10:14).

This means the responsibility of the preacher is at the same time both daunting and delightful. As Bob Fyall writes, 'every sermon becomes an *event* when we meet the Lord': the Holy Spirit takes the human words of frail and flawed people, to unfold the written word of God, so as to lead the congregation to the living Word, Christ Himself. There can be little more thrilling than to be a part of this! Hence every preacher who thus understands his task will want to do everything within his own power so as not to obscure the light and life of the divine Word behind preparation and presentation of his own that is banal or boring.

I am therefore delighted to introduce this book in which Bob Fyall encourages preachers to sense the wonderful privilege of a calling to be mouthpieces of the living and abiding Word, through which God's people encounter Christ together. He writes from a lifetime of experience – both in preaching and in training preachers – and with a passionate desire to help preachers lead others not only to know the Scriptures, but to know God, and love and serve Him more. To that end he shares many riches in these pages which will help preachers of all ages and stages think critically about their own preaching, and strive to live up to the task as faithfully and attractively as possible.

Bob's background as a teacher (and lover!) of English literature has given him voluminous knowledge few are blessed with, and, combined with his fine Hebrew scholarship, he has blessed many through his writings on the Old Testament narrative, poetry and prophecy. His love of C.S. Lewis, Shakespeare, and the poets in general, together with his extraordinary breadth of literary understanding, also brings a richness of approach to preaching which others will glean from with great profit.

I have been privileged to know Bob for many years, and over the last nearly two decades had the joy of working closely with him both at Cornhill Scotland (training Bible teachers) and as part of the Tron Church preaching team. I have learned an immense amount from him (about the Bible, theology, preaching, ministry, life – and Narnia!), and I have been blessed by his friendship and nourished by his preaching. So much of Bob's warm and engaging personality, as well as his learning, comes through in this book, and I know that all who read and ponder these pages will find much to enrich their own life and ministry, as I have. I warmly commend it and trust that it will lead many to 'come further up, come further in' to the joyful labour of speaking God's words to God's people.[1]

William J. U. Philip
Senior Minister, The Tron Church, Glasgow

---

1. To use one of Bob's favourite phrases from *The Last Battle*. Astonishingly, no quotes from Narnia appear in this book, so I am glad to supply one! (C. S. Lewis *is* of course mentioned.)

Preface

The inspiration for this book came from an off-the-cuff remark by Dick Lucas on one of his visits to Cornhill Scotland. 'Why,' he said, 'since we have so many excellent resources, commentaries and the like, is our preaching often so boring? Why don't you write a book about it?' At that time I didn't think there was enough material for a book, but for a number of years I did a lecture on the subject at Cornhill. More recently I returned to the idea and a number of people encouraged me to explore it further and this book is the result.

Much of what is said here is what I have been thinking and teaching and trying to exemplify over four decades in a range of contexts. My ministry began in a tough and unproductive situation in Bannockburn, Scotland, where the response was largely negative. After a few years, by a series of circumstances which I did not initiate, I went to Durham, England, initially to teach Old Testament at Cranmer Hall, St John's College. Later this became a joint ministry with what was then Claypath Church (now Christchurch) where a large student ministry developed. The teaching of the Bible in both contexts was very stimulating and rewarding as well as exhausting. Thereafter I became Director of Rutherford House (now Rutherford Centre for Reformed Theology) and preached widely as well as running preaching and other classes. Most recently I became Senior Tutor at the newly-formed Cornhill

Scotland and Associate Minister at the Tron Church, Glasgow. Thus for many years, I not only preached but was involved in training preachers. I also spoke at Christian Unions and other conferences. These twin emphases remain at the heart of my ministry in retirement. Preaching and theology belong together and their separation is detrimental, indeed destructive to both.

Underlying this book is the conviction that expository preaching is not only one of many good things for a church but the lifeblood of a healthy fellowship. Without it, other things, which may be good in themselves, can go badly wrong and fail to build anything of lasting worth. It is hard work and, particularly when results appear to be meagre, there is the temptation to try what seems to be more attractive and rewarding. This book is an attempt to encourage all of us to stick to the task and to be the best that we can be.

I hope to encourage preachers at all stages. Those just setting out need to be realistic and expect hard work, and often hard knocks, and I trust that they will find help here to keep going. Those longer on the road also need encouragement to keep pressing on believing that it is the proclamation of the Word of God which builds up the Church and reaches the world. Those, like me, who have retired from full-time ministry, need to keep on believing that in the Lord our labour has not been in vain, and to continue as opportunity and strength allow to carry on the work of the ministry and encourage younger people.

A number of friends and colleagues have read much of this book in draft and I am grateful for their support and helpful comments. They are Willie Philip (whom I also thank for the Introduction), David Jackman, Philip Stewart , Phil Copeland, Rupert Hunt Taylor, Garry Brotherston and Terry McCutcheon. I also thank Dick Lucas for suggesting the book and Christian Focus for agreeing to publish it. No words can express my thanks to my dear wife Thelma for her constant love, encouragement and support not only as I wrote this book but for all our years together.

As well as the people mentioned above, a book like this, drawing on my preaching and teaching over the years, has profited from sermons and talks listened to, books read and conversations recent and long ago. I have tried always to acknowledge the source of quotations and ideas from others. However, there are probably many times when comments or ideas have become so much part of my own thinking that I have forgotten the source. I apologise to anyone I have not acknowledged and am very grateful for the wealth of resources available to us (see especially Chapter 2). Ultimately, the Lord whom we all serve is the source of whatever is valuable in what we say or write. To God be the glory.

Bob Fyall
Glasgow
September 2022.

Chapter 1

A brittle crazie glass

Preaching does not always enjoy a good reputation and indeed the word is often used in a derogatory sense of pompous and boring speech. On the other hand, some have praised it in startling terms. C. H. Spurgeon said to his students, 'If God calls you to be a preacher, I would hate to see you stoop to be a king.' Others have spoken of preaching as the highest calling which anyone can be privileged to undertake. While agreeing with the latter statements, I suggest that they contain a danger. The danger is of over-valuing the preacher rather than preaching, the messenger more than the message. That, in our celebrity culture, can lead to the elevating of gurus whose every utterance is treated with reverence. Thus personality cults develop which honour humans more than God and place preachers on impossibly high pedestals.

That is why I have chosen the title 'A brittle crazie glass' from the sonnet 'The Windows' by the seventeenth-century preacher/poet George Herbert which shows both the weakness of the preacher and his utter dependence on the power of God as he is totally reliant on the light shining through him. In

Herbert's time, the word 'crazie'[1] did not mean exactly what it means now. Rather it develops the word 'brittle' as it means something like 'fragmented' or 'broken' (in contemporary English the nuance is still present in the term 'crazy paving'). It is through a fragile and broken vessel that the light comes. That is surely the same idea as in Paul's words, 'we have this treasure in jars of clay' (2 Cor. 4:7). These words, then as now, remain a challenge to the 'super apostles' he deals with later in the letter. The image of the glass in Herbert's poem refers particularly to a stained-glass window, dark in itself but glorious when the sun shines through it.

So we are brittle, feeble and broken to avoid thinking too highly of ourselves and yet be the channels of the grace of God. This theology of preaching flows from the fact that God is a speaking God whose words bring life (Gen.1). This Word is never empty, but like the seed, brings life and indeed ultimately leads to a new creation. Study Isaiah 55:10-13, a passage to which we shall return. What is truly amazing is that God has chosen humans to speak words which also do not return empty. A striking example of this is Acts 10 where Peter preaches to the Roman centurion Cornelius and others. 'While Peter was still speaking these words, the Holy Spirit fell on all who heard the word.' Notice the careful language. The Word of the Lord is not collapsed into the words of Peter, but the apostle's words are a necessary part of how the divine Word comes to those assembled. That is a picture of what happens when the Spirit takes our human words, uses them faithfully to unfold the written word and so leads us to the living Word, the Lord Christ Himself. Thus every sermon becomes an event when we meet the Lord.

The purpose of this book is to encourage brittle crazie glasses like myself to become confident in the God-given task while conscious of our own inadequacies. In a later chapter we will look at the preacher's personality and how this relates to our work. But it is worth asking, why are sermons often non-

---

1. I've kept the original spelling and also in the complete poem which can be found at the end of the chapter.

events and frankly often boring? Here are some suggestions; probably you can think of others yourself.

Why are sermons often non-events?

The first is the 'overloaded' sermon. Later we'll look at the necessary study and hard work, but that does not mean that we simply unload all we have discovered; there needs to be careful sifting of our material to make sure we have not obscured our main point by unnecessary detail. For sermons, on say the Old Testament history books, some background information is necessary but that is to be strictly subordinated to the message. In preaching on the later chapters of 2 Kings, for example, we will need to talk about Assyria and Babylon, but we should not give a potted history of both empires.

The next is the 'truncated' sermon which is the mirror image of the above. This is the kind of sermon where we know how we got from start to finish but everyone else doesn't have a clue. We must remember that the listeners will not have studied the text in the way we have and will need guidance.

Another type of sermon which can misfire is, 'I've done my theological training and I know the biblical languages.' Training is essential and we need to show the fruits of study but not parade them. Sometimes we will talk about possible alternative translations to the one we are using, but we need to be careful that we do not cause people to wonder if the translation they are using can be trusted.

Then there is the exegetical sermon which is content to 'explain' the passage without applying it. Incidentally, never say that you or someone else is going to explain the passage as if that were the whole act of preaching. We begin there, but there is so much else, and when we are dealing with poetry or apocalypse it is not even a helpful phrase. How do you 'explain' Isaiah 24, Song of Songs or Revelation 12?

An opposite of the above is, 'I say what's on my heart'; well, I hope we all do. But often that is an excuse for blessed thoughts strung together with anecdotes. Often that type of sermon is weak on exegesis and sloppy in application. The other thing is that that kind of sermon can often be produced with the bare minimum of preparation.

Another wrong method is taking passages out of context and saying things which may well be true but do not come from the passage. If we ignore context we can say anything we like. I recall a sermon on 2 Kings 4:8-10 where a rich woman in Shunem provides the prophet Elisha with a room at the top of her house. The sermon was called 'Upper storey living'. She provided a bed which speaks of rest; a table which suggests fellowship; a lamp which is the Word of God; and a chair to sit on to study it. Oh dear! The ministry of Elisha is ignored, and a few platitudes offered which have nothing to do with the context and trivialise the passage.

We shall explore how these and other inadequate models can be avoided. They all contain part of the truth: the need to pray and study and the vital importance of genuine engagement with the text and its application. However, it is important to set out some principles which underlie all our efforts and which flow from the Bible itself. These often are about bringing together things too often divorced and over-emphasising part of the truth at the expense of corresponding truth.

Diligent study and prayer

The first principle is that good preaching will be the result of careful study under the guidance of the Spirit. There is no contradiction between detailed study of commentaries and prayer asking for the Spirit's help. We all pray for such help in the actual service, but prayer must begin at a far earlier stage in the process. We can no more prepare a sermon without such help than we can preach it unaided. Nor should we imagine that prayer without study is all that is needed (illegitimately using such phrases as 'do not be anxious beforehand what you are to say,' Mark 13:11). If we are called to preach and have time and resources to study, the Spirit will help us in our weakness but not in our laziness. It is not that we do part of the work and the Spirit supplements this, but that our work is the sign that the Spirit is working. There will inevitably be times when we are not able to prepare as we would want, but we must never make exceptions into normal practice.

The whole Bible is profitable

The second principle is that the whole Bible is profitable and preachable. There is often a fear that unless we preach on a fairly narrow range of texts we will not be preaching the gospel. The whole Bible is the gospel and all of it leads to Christ. A ministry which majors on evangelistic addresses seldom either builds up believers or leads to conversions. Obviously, people must repent and believe, but not everyone begins that journey at the same point. A girl, who was brought to church by a Christian friend, was probably hoping for an evangelistic talk focussing on two ways to live. In fact, what she got was a sermon on Nahum. It was that which began her journey to faith. She came from a nominal churchgoing family where God was a cosy visitor at Christmas, perhaps also at Easter and harvest. That evening she confronted the God who created and is the Lord of history bringing about the rise and fall of nations. At some point later she believed that He was also her Saviour and Lord, but it was the initial contact with the Bible which the Spirit used to set her on the road.

Another way of putting the above is to allow the Bible to be the Bible, the written word which so fully and faithfully reveals the living Word. We do not have to make the Bible relevant; it is relevant, and our task is to show its relevance. This means moving from the 'what' to the 'so what?' Again this is easier in some passages than others. Sometimes this is because we have a limited idea of relevance confined to what we would *do* differently as a result. But often it is more of a question of how we would *be* different. Much of the Bible is about changing of attitudes which will lead to changed and Christlike behaviour. 'Be transformed by the renewal of your mind' (Rom.12:2) is far more than changing certain outward ways of behaving which is relatively easy.

Pastors and teachers

A third principle is that the pastor must be a teacher and the teacher must be a pastor. Ephesians 4:11 makes it plain that these are parts of one gift and not two separate gifts. Sometimes we hear that someone is not much of a preacher but is a great pastor. That won't do because preaching, feeding the flock, is at the heart of the pastor's ministry. It is equally true that if someone has the reputation of being a great preacher in terms of oratorical skills and yet does not care for people then he will not move hearts or change lives. This is true not only of preachers who lead a particular congregation but of all who preach whether regularly or occasionally. Indeed, having taught at theological college, I believe that the teacher in that setting is only truly effective when there is pastoral concern for students.

We must believe in our hearts what we are preaching

That leads to a fourth principle, perhaps the most important of all which is that the preacher must believe, in the fullest sense of the word, what he is preaching. This means preaching to ourselves. It is not a question of a religious expert giving instruction to inferiors but the bringing of the Word of God to both preachers and hearers for both to respond. Later we shall explore the preacher's personality and style because not everyone expresses themselves in the same way and different kinds of people show emotion in different styles. In the eighteenth century, George Whitefield was well known for his oratorical gifts and dramatic style which impressed many who did not believe his message. The great Shakespearian actor/manager, David Garrick, often heard Whitefield and said, 'I would give a hundred guineas to be able to say "O" the way that Mr Whitefield does.' Perhaps even more surprising was the experience of David Hume, the Scottish sceptic and philosopher. One evening a friend met him as he was hurrying over London Bridge and asked where he was going; 'To hear Whitefield,' Hume replied. 'But you don't believe any of that,' said the friend. 'No,' Hume said, 'but Whitefield does.' That is so impressive, Whitefield does. We are not Whitefield, but in our own situations and personalities what is needed is a conviction and certainty which cannot be denied.

Keep reading the Bible

All of these principles assume an increasing familiarity with the Bible. One thing which is all too easy for preachers and teachers is to use the Bible only as a quarry for sermons, lectures and writing. Over twenty years ago I realised that I was not reading the Bible. That sounds nonsense. At that time I had a joint appointment as pastor of a church and lecturer at a theological college and I was studying, teaching and preaching daily. The trouble was that I was not reading the Bible except to prepare sermons and lectures and books. I have since then used the Bible reading plan first devised by Robert Murray McCheyne and have found that to be at the centre of my spiritual life. So, preachers, read the Bible. The particular method does not matter as long as you explore the whole biblical landscape regularly. That does not mean that your regular preparation for preaching is less important, but it roots that in regular Bible reading habits. Indeed much of good preaching flows from reading the Bible with regard to its genres and emphases.

A good model : Ecclesiastes 12:9-14[2]

Since this book is about encouraging good preaching, it is structured around the portrait of the Preacher in Ecclesiastes 12:9-14, a concise but remarkably comprehensive picture of

---

2. 'Besides being wise, the Preacher also taught the people knowledge, weighing and studying and arranging many proverbs with great care. The Preacher sought to find words of delight, and uprightly he wrote words of truth.

'The words of the wise are like goads, and like nails firmly fixed are the collected sayings; they are given by one Shepherd. My son, beware of anything beyond these. Of making many books there is no end, and much study is a weariness of the flesh.

'The end of the matter; all has been heard. Fear God and keep his commandments, for this is the whole duty of man. For God will bring every deed into judgment, with every secret thing, whether good or evil (Ecclesiastes 12:9-14).

both the style and content of preaching. The next chapter will be a survey of how we are where we are. My own ministry has been in Scotland and England, and I do not have first-hand experience of the situation elsewhere, but I hope that it will be of interest to those in different situations. After all, once we have made the necessary adjustments for different times and places, the Word of God in its eternal truth presents the same challenges as it always did. The spirit in which we approach our work is expressed beautifully in the Collect for the second Sunday of Advent in the Book of Common Prayer:

> Blessed Lord, who hast caused all holy Scriptures to be written for our learning: Grant that we may in such wise hear them, read, mark, learn and inwardly digest them, that by patience and comfort of thy holy Word, we may embrace and ever hold fast the blessed hope of everlasting life, which thou hast given us in our Saviour Jesus Christ. Amen.

Here is the complete poem by George Herbert:

The Windows

LORD, how can man preach thy eternal word?
He is a brittle crazie glass:
Yet in thy temple thou dost him afford
This glorious and transcendent place,
To be a window, through thy grace.
But when thou dost anneal in glass thy storie,
Making thy life to shine within
The holy Preachers; then the light and glorie
Most rev'rend grows and more doth win:
Which else shows watrish, bleak and thin.
Doctrine and life, colours and light, in one
When they combine and mingle, bring
A strong regard and awe: but speech alone
Doth vanish like a flaring thing,
And in the eare, not conscience ring.

Chapter 2

How we got where we are

Like everything else, preaching does not happen in a vacuum and the purpose of this chapter is to explore the background of today's preaching and the resources for preachers. This is not an attempt at even a summary history of preaching but a brief survey of developments in the period from the end of the Second World War. Since then, an unprecedented wealth of resources has become available, and a wise use of such resources will help us to avoid being boring.

There are two limitations I want to make clear at this point. The first is that the concentration is on England and Scotland. This is not being parochial; rather this is where my own ministry has been, and I am not qualified to speak of other places except at second hand. Also, preaching, although styles and idioms will vary from place to place and from time to time, is of universal significance and the basic practice is not tied to particular circumstances.

The second is that the concentration will be on major figures noted as powerful preachers. Inevitably they are better known, and fuller information is available about their ministries. We have already noted how we must not exalt preachers into gurus and try to imitate them. However, learning from them is not only desirable but necessary. Doubtless there are and have been many faithful and inspirational preachers whose work is not so well known. In the end it is the Lord who will assess both the famous and the little known and that is the verdict which matters. However, there is much we can learn from those into whose labours we have entered and who made, and in some cases continue to make, a significant impact.

Two particular matters call for comment: the revival of expository preaching and the parallel flourishing of evangelical biblical and theological scholarship. We shall explore both and make some comments on their legacy. Here, as in so many other areas, the explosion of the internet has made more resources than ever available bringing with it the need to discriminate wisely (more of this later).

The revival of expository preaching

A feature of the Reformation was a flood of expository sermons with the likes of Calvin, Luther and Melanchthon preaching systematically through biblical books as well as writing commentaries. That tradition was somewhat lost in succeeding centuries. Not that there was no faithful preaching, but that figures such as Charles Spurgeon tended to preach on texts rather than unfolding books and sections of the Bible in continuous exposition. We'll return to this point later.

The English scene

A significant figure here was the former doctor, Martyn Lloyd Jones, particularly in his ministry at Westminster Chapel, London from 1939 to 1969, having earlier ministered in Wales.[1] He preached truly massive series on Romans and Ephesians which were a veritable feast of biblical truth, but such length prevented him giving many other expositions of biblical books, particularly from the Old Testament. This was not altogether a helpful model for those of lesser gifts in very different situations.

---

1. See the two-volume biography by Iain Murray: Vol.1 *The First Forty years (1899-1939)*, (Banner of Truth: Edinburgh, 1982); Vol. 2 *The Fight of Faith (1939- 1981)*, (Banner of Truth, 1991).

Also in London there was the hugely influential ministry of John Stott.[2] His ministry at All Souls established expository preaching as the regular practice. Later he developed a worldwide ministry which has continuing influence. He worked closely with Billy Graham and took part in countless student missions. His style was lucid, and he had particular gifts of biblical analysis shown in his commentaries as well as his sermons. A further legacy is his editing of the *New Testament Bible Speaks Today* series (Alec Motyer edited the Old Testament series) which continue to be of particular help to preachers. Alec Motyer continued his preaching and writing to the great benefit of the Church until his death in his nineties. Both men contributed some of the volumes themselves, as well as much else.

The dispute between Lloyd Jones and Stott in 1966 over whether evangelicals should leave mainline denominations is well known. This is not the place for yet another account of that meeting, except to say that it is a thousand pities they were not able to work more closely together.

A further hugely influential development took place in 1961 when Dick Lucas was called to St Helen's Bishopsgate in the City of London. He immediately set about establishing expository preaching, not only in the Sunday services but also in the Tuesday lunchtime services, attended by many from the business community. The church grew and became increasingly influential. The Proclamation Trust was founded in 1986 to support and develop Dick Lucas' ministry.

An important development was the founding of the Cornhill Training Course in 1991. Even good theological colleges were not providing extensive training in preaching and something which placed the emphasis on biblical exposition was badly needed. David Jackman, coming from a fruitful expository

---

2. Another two-parter: Timothy Dudley Smith, *The Making of a Leader,* (IVP); *A Global Ministry,* (IVP), 2001. For Stott's own view on preaching, see his *I believe in Preaching,* (IVP, 1982).

ministry in Southampton, was appointed Director.[3] The influence of Cornhill has extended to other countries (later we'll look at Cornhill Scotland), and many have gone from such training to exercise helpful and flourishing ministries in many places.

Doubtless, other names and situations could be mentioned but there is no attempt to be comprehensive here but rather to indicate the growth and development of expository preaching and give credit where credit is due.

The Scottish scene

Meanwhile, in Scotland, parallel developments were taking place. The pioneer there was William Still (1911-1997) who spent his whole ministry at Gilcomston South Church in Aberdeen. Beginning with an aggressively evangelistic ministry, he turned to expository preaching not only to build up believers but as a more effective way of winning outsiders. This, at first, especially when he replaced Saturday night rallies with a prayer meeting, led to reduced numbers but that was temporary, and the ministry grew both numerically and in its wider influence.[4]

One significant outcome of his ministry was the calling of many men to similar kinds of ministry throughout Scotland. The earliest of these was James Philip (1922-2009) who ministered first in the village of Gardenstown in the north of Scotland, a ministry which was marked by many conversions, and of others being called to Christian service. His later ministry in Holyrood Abbey in Edinburgh was one of the most significant of the later part of the twentieth century and its

---

3. See *When God's Voice is Heard: Essays on Preaching presented to Dick Lucas*, eds. David Jackman and Christopher Green, (IVP, 1995).

4. See *Pulpit and People: Essays in honour of William Still on his seventy fifth birthday*; eds. Nigel Cameron and Sinclair Ferguson, (Rutherford House Books, Edinburgh, 1986). See also his *The Work of the Pastor*, 1st edition, 1984, edited by Sinclair Ferguson in 2010 and published by Christian Focus, 2010, 2011. Also, his autobiography, *Dying to Live*, (Christian Focus, 1991).

influence is still felt.[5] James' brother George had an influential ministry in Sandyford Henderson Church in Glasgow. One of the more notable preachers was Eric Alexander, first in Newmilns in Ayrshire, then at St George's Tron in Glasgow. His ministry also reached widely, particularly though his many preaching tours in America. Other gifted preachers also ministered in most parts of the country, and this continues to the present day. This historical sketch makes no claim to be complete but rather to demonstrate how there was a significant revival of preaching and to indicate some of the major figures and developments.

The flourishing of evangelical scholarship

This was another feature of the post-World War Two years. Again this is a sketch of some significant figures and developments. The work of evangelical scholars gave important impetus to the production of resources which encouraged the expository task and helped to give preachers confidence in the reliability of the Bible.

The pioneers

Probably the most significant figure was F.F. Bruce (1910-1990),[6] a Scot who spent most of his professional life in England. He was a man of enormous erudition who began his career lecturing in Greek first at Edinburgh University and then at Leeds University. He moved quickly to Biblical Studies, being Head of Department first at Sheffield University and later at Manchester University. He produced many books: commentaries on much of the New Testament as well as works on the canon and on the historicity of the New Testament. He was not a particularly scintillating speaker or writer, but his work was marked by great clarity and was free from jargon. His influence was worldwide and encouraged many others to pursue sound biblical scholarship. He was a scholar rather

---

5.   The bulk of James Philip's sermons and Bible studies can be found on the website of the Tron Church, Glasgow. The link is www.tron.church/ Resources.

6.   See Tim Grass, *F. F. Bruce: A Life*,)Paternoster, 2011).

than a preacher, but as a lifelong member of the Christian Brethren he preached frequently.

In the Old Testament field, Donald Wiseman (1918-2010) was a significant influence. He was an Assyriologist and worked both at the University of London and the British Museum. Much of his work was in translating Assyrian texts and also field archaeology. However, he was also a committed biblical scholar, writing the Tyndale commentary on 1 and 2 Kings, as well as being a translator of the New International Version. He also wrote many books and articles defending the historicity and reliability of the Old Testament, including work on Daniel. Like Bruce he was widely respected by those who did not share his views.

Later developments

One important consequence of the revival of evangelical biblical scholarship was the founding of Tyndale House in Cambridge in 1944.[7] This was, and is, a residential library devoted to scholarship at the highest level. Many well-known scholars have studied and lectured there, and this continues to the present day. Bruce and Wiseman were involved early in this venture and much helpful material continues to be produced there. One figure who has been particularly associated with Tyndale House is the scholar/preacher Don Carson who still exercises an influential ministry. All these developments continue to be significant, and we turn now to making some comments.

Reflections on our inheritance

We are in a time when a uniquely wide range of resources is available to us as we set about the task of preaching, and it is important that we use these wisely and in a spirit of eagerness to learn.

---

7.   See T. A. Noble, *Tyndale House and Fellowship: the First Sixty Years*, (IVP, 2006).

Gratitude

First, we are grateful to God for providing so much helpful material from which we can profit. This is a good attitude as it encourages us to approach our study in a spirit of humility and a sense of discovery. The Lord gives teachers who open our eyes to new things in His unchanging Word and help us to avoid being boringly predictable. Of course, preaching must be predictable in the sense that it is the one authoritative gospel we present. However, we must not be trite and mundane in our presentation and thus ensure there is the right kind of unpredictability which will keep people awake.

Discrimination

Balancing the above, we must remember that only one Book is inerrant. This is particularly important when we are reading or listening to our favourite teachers. Our example is the Bereans of whom Luke wrote, 'they received the word with all eagerness, examining the Scriptures daily to see if these things were so.' Here is a true humility as they eagerly listen to the Word, but a real discernment as they test what they hear by Scripture. When the Bible is taught clearly and powerfully the listeners are helped to become Bible students themselves. Good preaching will not lead people to say, 'O that's so clever, I could never do that,' but will rather encourage them to read their Bibles with increasing diligence and enthusiasm. Open mindedness and a commitment to the truth are both necessary to avoid sterility and unbridled speculation.

There will be selectivity in what we read. The Preacher warns that not everything written is profitable (Ecc. 12:12). Nor is a commentary good simply because it carries the label 'evangelical'. Likewise, we can learn much from people of different standpoints particularly on such matters as the biblical languages. When using commentaries we do not need to accept everything on trust but judge them by their faithfulness to elucidating the text of Scripture.

Keep on learning

This is a lifetime commitment. As long as the Lord gives us health and opportunity we must remain students with a realisation that there is far more than we will ever master in a lifetime. This is obvious when we are setting out, but the vision can become dimmed. As we continue, we build more and more material, but even when we are drawing on such we need to re-engage with it and apply it to present situations. Our minds need to be alert and teachable, for only as we continue to learn can we effectively teach others. Neither throw away your old notes nor simply regurgitate them. Keep on reading big books which expand the mind and remain open to new vistas.

Use commentaries wisely

Commentaries are not directly a quarry for sermons and should be used with discretion and wisdom. At an early stage of our work on a text it is useful to consult a detailed heavyweight commentary which provides information on language and background and helps us to avoid sermons based on faulty translations or inadequate knowledge of background. The New International Commentaries on the Old Testament and the New Testament (published by Eerdmans) are helpful in this respect. As in all series, some volumes are more useful than others. Having worked extensively on Isaiah, I have found John Oswalt particularly helpful (Vol. 1, 1987; Vol. 2 1999). The Tyndale Commentaries (published by IVP) do the same kind of thing on a smaller scale. Earlier volumes are being replaced, although not always improved. On a larger scale is the Word Commentary. It is difficult to see how some of the volumes deserve the label 'evangelical', although there are some good volumes (I have found the two on Hebrews valuable). As always, use what is helpful.

There are also various series which are more directly helpful to the preacher. One of these is The Bible Speaks Today (IVP). As with the Tyndale Commentaries, some of the earlier volumes are being replaced. These move from exposition to application and the best volumes are very good indeed. Proclamation Trust in conjunction with Christian Focus are producing Teachers' Guides which are neither straight commentaries nor collections of sermons but aim to help preachers to move from the 'what?' of the text to the 'so what?' These volumes are best used after your main work of exegesis is done. They do not present an unalterable way in which the text is to be preached but try to open fruitful lines of application and show how experienced preachers have approached the text.

There are the commentaries of great expositors of the past such as Luther and Calvin with all their spiritual depth and profound insights. When using these, we must remember that they spoke living truth in the language and idiom of their time as we must do in ours. Commentaries are like cookery books. They help to provide tasty ingredients for our kitchen (study), but the secret lies in blending these ingredients skilfully and attractively to produce nourishing meals.

Aim to be comprehensive
Put another way, do not leave any part of the Bible out, because all of it is profitable. With all the resources available, all parts of Scripture have useful commentary, some more than others, but even less familiar books now have resources for understanding. There is not any part of the Bible which should be neglected. Obviously, there will be appropriate balance in the amount of time spent on various books and some will be preached several times, but all Scripture is given to present Christ and build Christian character. To return to the food metaphor, provide a balanced diet. Regular preaching to one congregation is like feeding the family, balance is provided over time. A one-off sermon is more like inviting people for a meal where balance is attempted in the different courses. All of us are different and each of us is more drawn to some parts of the Bible than others but we must guard against a natural inclination becoming a governing principle and make

sure we do not neglect or undervalue those parts we are less attracted by.

Trust in God and keep your powder dry

These words, attributed to Oliver Cromwell, can also be applied to our preaching. The dry powder is the matters to be discussed such as knowledge of text, hard work, diligent preparation, wide reading and the like which have a part to play in this great task. Yet without the power of God these will achieve little. A good biblical example would be Nehemiah trusting God to protect the builders and yet posting guards with spears in hand (Neh. 4:18-23). We do not labour believing we can build the wall in our own strength. Yet our work is a sign that we are truly trusting the Lord to bless. In earlier days, the phrase 'let go and let God' was often used as a mantra to lead to fruitfulness and maturity. There is truth in the statement in that only the grace of God can transform us, but if we then assume that we do nothing then we slide into self-indulgence. I once met a man who said that he did not prepare a passage for preaching but prepared himself. How he did that without engaging with Scripture was not made clear. Surely, we need the words of Paul which apply to preaching as well as to all other aspects of our Christian lives, 'work out your own salvation with fear and trembling, for it is God who works in you, both to will and to work for his good pleasure' (Phil. 2:12-13). Use the resources with prayer and thanksgiving, and trust God to bless our work.

Chapter 3

How shall they hear?

J. I. Packer said, 'there is no truer or happier way to describe the Scriptures of both Testaments ... than as God *preaching*.'[1] This is because God speaks through it not only to give us information but also to call for a response of faith and transformed living. Thus, if we are to be faithful to the Word of God in our preaching we must follow the Bible as the Holy Spirit takes these words and applies them to ourselves and others. This will mean realising that the whole Bible is preachable, a point to which we will return. Sometimes this teaching is direct as in the prophets and New Testament writers. Other times, as in narrative, it is more indirect but nonetheless has a powerful message. To take perhaps the most striking example: the Book of Esther does not mention God and has no reference to any of Israel's rites apart from fasting, yet by brilliant narration and powerful description deconstructs human power. The king and his council, after solemn conclave and excessive drinking, succeed in coming up with an idea that any male chauvinist could have thought of immediately (Esther 1:20).

---

1.   'Preaching as Biblical Interpretation' in *Honouring the Written Word of God: The Collected Shorter Writings of J. I. Packer.* Vol. 3, (Paternoster Press, 1999), p. 319.

But first a word about preaching itself. Even amongst those committed to the supreme authority of the Bible, preaching is often seen as only one among other ways of presenting the truth. In one sense this is true, in that small group studies, informal presentations to young people, and writing are important ways of communicating. Indeed, in the contemporary world of Twitter and the like, long monologues are seen as off-putting. There are two problems here. One is that people's intelligence is insulted by assuming they are incapable of listening to anything other than soundbites. The other is that often that argument is supported by taking bad (indeed boring) examples of preaching and comparing these with attractive examples of more informal styles of communicating.

Further, it is often pointed out that a passage often referred to in advocating the primacy of preaching is based on an inadequate translation. 1 Corinthians 1:21, in the KJV, reads: 'it pleased God by the foolishness of preaching to save them that believe.' More accurately, the verse would be rendered as 'the foolishness of what was preached' (NIV) or 'the folly of what we preach' (ESV), placing the emphasis on the substance, the message itself, rather than the way it is conveyed. But that is to miss the point. Paul could have used other words such as 'reasoning', 'debating' and the like, but he chooses to use the term that suggests authoritative declaration of the Word in the power of the Spirit.

So let us turn to the Preacher, the author of Ecclesiastes, and especially to the Epilogue of the book (Eccles. 12:9-14). First, though, to see that in context, it is important to say something about the book as a whole. The author, or someone passing on his words, uses the title *Qoheleth* which is a term for someone who calls together an assembly (*qahal, Greek ecclesia*) to address it. The word has no exact English equivalent, and it is variously rendered as Preacher, Teacher, Lecturer or Professor. Many studies of the book simply use the Hebrew word. Perhaps the Americanism, 'Mr Preacher', catches something of its flavour.

'Son of David, king in Jerusalem' places him at the heart of Israel's life, but his book, as is characteristic of Wisdom literature, raises profound questions about that life. Some believe that the author is Solomon himself, but in 1:16 he speaks of all who reigned in Jerusalem before him, and only David did before Solomon. More likely it is someone assuming Solomon's mantle and asking if he had Solomon's opportunities, wisdom, power, wealth and status, could he make a success of this mortal life 'under the sun' or 'under heaven'.

The heart of his message is that 'under the sun' or 'under heaven' everything is *hebel*. The word means futile, empty, meaningless, wind, vapour. Interestingly the word is used of idols e.g. Jeremiah 10:15: 'They (idols) are worthless, a work of delusion.' Thus a lifestyle, however attractive and appealing, which has horizons that are limited by time and space is doomed to be eventually meaningless. This applies to all circumstances, whether joyful or sad.

In earlier days I emphasised the importance of this book to those who were not Christians, and that is true because the 'God-shaped blank' in the human heart (3:11) cannot be filled apart from Christ Himself. But we must not limit the book to that because Christians still face *hebel*, which will only be finally removed in the new creation. A recurring emphasis is that death brings to an end every human activity, whether wise or foolish.

The Epilogue (12:9-14) makes clear the underlying message of the book and shows the full meaning of earlier passages. 12:1-8 is a moving and poignant picture of the process of dying and the coming of death itself, and this concludes with the author's final mention of *hebel*. But beyond the grave there is new life, and this mortal life is given for us to use well and wisely so that we can be ready for the life to come. As we look at the Epilogue we shall see that this is not an 'orthodox' rewriting of the book to make it 'safe', but rather it is showing us that what is to come is already anticipated in this world if we look beyond it. With that in mind we look now at its concise but comprehensive view of preaching which changes thinking and attitude. Here we will make a brief survey of the passage because these points will be developed later in this book. The depiction of preaching here develops in four movements.

The character of the Preacher (9a). The preacher needs to be wise with wisdom which comes from God. However, wisdom is not an end in itself; it is given to be passed on and is for the benefit of the hearers. This will increase people's knowledge of what is good and valuable and if humbly accepted it will lead to wisdom.

The work of the Preacher (9b-10). True preaching will need hard work and diligent sifting of material. No preacher can remain fresh and interesting without being a lifelong student. 'Weighing' not only implies careful selection but care in presentation. 'Proverbs' is not limited to sayings, but includes parables, questions, story and many other literary forms. There is not only solid truth but imaginative and skilful delivery. Truth and beauty belong together.

The inspiration of the Preacher (11-13). The above is true of any public speaking, but here is a more fundamental issue: where do the words come from? They are 'given', and thus their content is non-negotiable, which in no way diminishes the need for study. Sinclair Ferguson said, 'The preacher creates the *sermon*, he does not create the *message*.'[2] When we realise this we will work even harder because the words must not be thoughtlessly delivered. The use of the title 'Shepherd' for God is significant and will be explored later. Suffice it to say that the twin ideas of feeding and guarding are at the heart of preaching. Here the 'words of the wise' are applied more widely than those of *Qoheleth* himself.

Such words will provoke to action (goads) and will be firmly fixed (nails), surely a true blend of productive behaviour and stability. This is coupled with a warning against the wrong kind of teaching. Not everything written or spoken is valuable

---

2. 'Exegesis' in *Preaching*, ed. Samuel T. Logan Jr., (Evangelical Press, 1985), p. 292.

and deserving careful study. The words of the Shepherd must be the touchstone of other works (more of this later). That is why we need the whole Bible.

The message of the Preacher (13-14). 'All has been heard' does not mean that the entire truth is contained in Ecclesiastes, but rather that the writer wants us to see that his conclusion leads to this point. Here we have two great summary verses which encapsulate the truth and summarise the continuing message of the whole Bible, especially its teaching about humanity and God.

The first truth is what it means to be truly human. There is no word for 'duty' in the Hebrew text. 'This is the whole of humanity', of what it means to be a human being. 'Fear God' suggests the true spirit of reverence and awe which we must have as we realise how incomparably greater He is than the whole created order. This is combined with a true obedience. Fear will keep us from a legalistic and joyless attitude, and obedience will keep us from a vague mysticism.

The second truth shows that *hebel* is not the end because God the eternal Judge will assess everything. In the light of eternity what we do in this world matters. 'Good' and 'evil' remind us of Genesis 3 and the Fall which brought *hebel* into the world, but also of the promised Saviour and the renewal of creation itself.

These points will be developed in later chapters but some comments about the importance of this Epilogue, especially in relation to our preaching, would be helpful here. *Qoheleth* (12:9) is concerned to pass on the words of the Shepherd and in the book he has exemplified true preaching as well as making this explicit in the Epilogue.

First, he is a realist and will give no comfort to those who want to live in a fantasy land. This world is fallen and under a curse and thus everything is futile if our horizons are limited to the visible and the temporal. Thus, trying to find true fulfilment in relationships, work, leisure and achievements of all kinds is doomed to failure (see e.g. 2:21; 4:13-16; 6:12; 9:11-12). The grim spectre of death haunts every human life, and this is particularly emphasised in 3:18-20. These verses, which speak of animal and human death and disappearance, is not the Old Testament denying that there is life after death; but rather they underline the fact that if our perspective is limited to this life then there is truly no difference in the death of an animal and a human. As preachers we must not give false hopes and build up expectations for this life which this world can never satisfy.

Second, this realism must be balanced by another emphasis. This world is indeed fallen but it is still beautiful and wonderful. Moonlit skies, autumn woodlands, summer meadows and the changing seasons all bear witness to the unfailing goodness of the Creator. Thus we are not to have a suspicion and indeed rejection of the many blessings of this earthly life. We must not encourage a joyless legalism which rejects the arts, good food and wine, leisure activities and above all the joys of human love. When we realise that we can truly enjoy all these things as foretastes of the fuller joy of the new creation, then we can see this life in its true perspective. Our preaching needs to reflect this balance of realism and hope, in the biblical sense of that word. *Qoheleth* does not despise beauty and pleasure but talks of their passing nature, although always aware that in the world to come such joys will be unimaginably greater and eternal. Some wonderful words from Margaret Clarkson capture something of the excitement of that world with bodies perfectly suited to it:

O, resurrection body,
young, radiant, vibrant, free,
with powers unthought, undreamed of –
how rich your joys shall be!
Through endless years to marvel,
design, create, explore,
in resurrection wonder
to worship, serve, adore.[3]

---

3.   From 'In resurrection bodies, like Jesus' very own' (1987).

Preach that and people who think of heaven as some kind of vast concert hall where eternity is spent strumming harps will see how far more exciting the new creation will be.

Third, we must preach big subjects. Implicit throughout the book and explicit in the Epilogue is *Qoheleth's* concentration on the great truths of God and humanity, life and death, and eternity and judgment, which must be at the centre of our preaching. We do not need to be bored by platitudes even if they are biblically based. If I want to hear platitudes I can go for a haircut or take a ride in a taxi. That does not mean trying to be original,[4] but it does mean expressing the truth through the personality God has given you. We will explore this further when we look at predictable and unpredictable preaching. Suffice it to say that preaching must be faithful to the text but avoid the kind of predictability that means listeners who are still awake will know what you are going to say next. Also avoid the kind of unpredictability which uses the text as a springboard for our own ideas.

Ultimately, faithfulness to Scripture will save us from both errors. We will be predictable in that what we preach must be the Bible itself without either taking away from it or adding to it. Taking away from it is the error of liberalism which rejects any truth which does not suit contemporary thinking. Adding to it is the error of legalism which adds demands that the Bible itself does not make.

The task is daunting, but the Holy Spirit is ready to help us in our weakness and He who inspired the Scriptures is the One who helps us to understand and apply them.

---

4. C.S. Lewis in a sermon, 'The Weight of Glory' said, 'No man who values originality will ever be original.'

Chapter 4

A worker who does not need to be ashamed

These words of Paul in 2 Timothy 2:15 remind us that preaching is hard work; not that hard work on its own will be enough, but it is the essential foundation of the whole enterprise. Cutting corners and trying to find more apparently productive ways of operating which promise quicker rewards are always tempting. The opposite temptation is to regard our preparation as itself meritorious, and something will be said at the end of the chapter about the danger of being a workaholic. We shall look at preparation, planning and wider reading.

The first necessity is to read and study the text. This is obvious, but often given lip service rather than practised. Before we can preach, we must allow the text to grip us and we must be alive to its nuances and depths. Reading aloud is important because this often brings out what the text is emphasising. We all have our preferred text, but it is useful to compare different versions or, better still, consult the original languages. Not everyone will know these, but there are many helps available. You do not need to be an expert, but it is always better to try to get some acquaintance with the languages and understand something of their power. Always, as already mentioned in Chapter 1, our reading must be like that of

Qoheleth who became wise himself before he imparted what he had learned to others. The work of preparation is never simply an academic exercise, but it is part of our spiritual life and offered to the Lord.

The next stage (and these are not mechanical steps but guidelines) is the use of commentaries and other resources. Commentaries are not meant to do our sermon work for us. Useful series such as the Teachers' Guide to Biblical Books should be used when we have done our main exegetical work and not as a substitute for it. The use of commentaries is first to give accurate information about language, grammar and sufficient background, which will prevent us building sermons on inaccurate understanding, as well as often providing penetrating insights. Historical and geographical background is very important, but must be used sparingly to help a fuller understanding of the passage.

An example illustrates this point. The story of how King Sennacherib of Assyria devastated Judah but failed to capture Jerusalem is told in 2 Kings 18 and 19, Isaiah 36 and 37, and more briefly in 2 Chronicles 32. The climax of the story, the destruction of the Assyrian army and Sennacherib's hasty return home, is given in only two verses (2 Kings 19:35-36 and the identical Isaiah 37:36-37, while 2 Chronicles 32 describes it in similar words). How does this compare with extra-biblical accounts? Sennacherib's own account speaks of the campaign against Judah, and in particular the destruction of Judah's second city, Lachish, which was portrayed on huge wall carvings (now in the British Museum) on the walls of one of the main rooms in his principal palace in Nineveh. There is no account of the fall of Jerusalem. Why all this fuss about a faraway town which probably no one in Nineveh had heard of? Surely it was propaganda to disguise the fact that he had failed in his main objective. Assyrian spin doctors did not report defeats. Another account is by the Greek historian Herodotus who said that a bubonic plague broke out in the Assyrian camp destroying huge numbers of the army. All accounts agree that Jerusalem did not fall.

But that information is not only an interesting detail of ancient history but a revelation about the God who works in history. Herodotus' account of plague is a perfectly reasonable natural explanation of the event, given the insanitary conditions of campaigning, but it does not answer the 'why' question. The Angel of Yahweh had again, as at the Exodus, visited and protected God's people. So, when using background, always be alert to its spiritual significance. The details mentioned above give confidence that the events happened as the Bible described them, but that alone does not lead to saving faith or growth in grace. We need to see how everything is related to the character of God and His purposes.

But there is more. As always, theology must lead to doxology. Just as the Exodus was celebrated in the great song of Moses (Exod.15), a song which exalts Yahweh above the godlets of the nations (Exod. 15:11), so this deliverance is also celebrated in song. The Psalms continually celebrate the greatness of God and His mighty acts, and two in particular, the great Zion Psalms 46 and 48, almost certainly reflect this episode and crystallise its experience for all future generations.

Psalm 46 speaks of God's power over the turbulent creation as well as His activity in history. The river (v. 4) is the river of Eden (Gen. 2:10) and of the new Jerusalem (Rev. 22:1) which brings abundant life and symbolises the presence of God in His city. But there is probably a reference to the Gihon spring which Hezekiah diverted to bring water into the city in case of a prolonged siege (2 Chron. 32:3-4). Also the little detail, 'God will help her at break of day' (v. 5 NIV) is exactly what happened as a terrifying night passed and on the next morning the fearful Assyrian army had 'melted like snow in the glance of the Lord'.[1] But this goes far beyond its time and place to every time and place because Hezekiah's God is our God.

Likewise Psalm 48 focusses on the eternal security of Zion whose protection is God Himself who destroys His enemies,

---

1. From Byron's poem, 'The destruction of Sennacherib.'

echoing Psalm 2. Again the praise of Yahweh is not confined to His temple but reaches to the ends of the earth (v. 10). In spite of enemy attacks, Zion is still there (vv. 12-13). The proud Assyrians had thought they would take her treasure and pull down her walls (Isa. 33:17-18), but they had vanished, and beyond that the true Zion can never be destroyed.

I hope this example has given some help as we start our preparation. We are thinking of a whole experience where not only the spoken word but the prayers and items of praise help to shape our response. Reading, commentaries and background material need to be used so that by the end of the service hearts are bowed before God in wonder, love and praise.

Now we have done our initial preparation and collected a mass of material to feed the flock. Even as when we invite people to our home for lunch or dinner, we do not place the ingredients on the dining room table but blend them together to make a satisfying meal, so we do not unload what is on our desk to the lectern. What we do now is prepare a sermon outline or plan. This is where we need imagination and creativity not to read between the lines but to select, arrange and 'find just the right words' (Eccles.12:10 NIV). In a later chapter we shall explore further the use of words and their impact.

It is often said that the typical evangelical sermon is 'three points and a poem'. Why just one? Again we should not despise the three pointer too readily. Three is a useful number which provides a guide and a sense of progress to the journey. Again this is not a mechanical rule but is a help for listeners to remember the essence of a sermon. It gives the preacher clarity and direction.

One very important aspect of planning is analysis of the passage, not least because it is vital that we do not end up with Job or Philippians in my own words. We already have been given God's own words and our task is to bring out and apply their meaning. The title of the sermon must give a brief statement of the overall message and the headings must give a concise summary of the meaning of the passage. Let me give an example of sermons preached twenty years apart on 2 and 3 John. The first set largely summarised the content, whereas the second attempted to bring out the thrust of both letters. Here is the first attempt:

2 John – Walking in the truth

Introduction – circumstances of the letter
> The Greeting (vv. 1-3) – Importance of love and truth
> The Main Message (vv. 4-11) – The danger of false teachers
> Final Greetings (vv. 12-13) – Genuine affection.

3 John – Worthy of God

Introduction – again circumstances
> Address to Gaius (vv. 1-3) – Care for physical and spiritual well being
> The case of Diotrephes (vv. 9-10) – Danger of bullying
> The case of Demetrius (vv. 11-12) – Case of Demetrius
> Final Greetings (vv. 13-14)

While that outline indeed follows the pattern of the letters, it simply summarises the content. No doubt much that was helpful was said but in a somewhat pedestrian way. The headings sound rather like the agenda for a meeting.

The second attempt makes more of tracing the underlying meaning and tries to show both the contrast and comparison of the two letters. Also the twenty intervening years hopefully added spiritual maturity. Here is the second attempt:

2 John – Recognising the fake

Introduction – Both letters addressed to a group of churches with a particular link with the apostle John to help in recognising false and true teachers.

How do we recognise the fake?

They present a false Christ (esp. v. 7) – the language is strong – 'deceiver' and antichrist – deny incarnation, salvation and true fellowship.

They offer false progress (esp. vv. 8-9) – pretend we can move on from Christ – 'does not continue and runs ahead'.

They come under false pretences (esp. vv. 10-11) – they are often charming people but do not give them platforms.

3 John – Welcoming the genuine

Introduction – No retreat from truth but warning not to retreat into a legalistic mindset.

How do we recognise the genuine? (vv. 1-8)

Faithful to and continuing in the truth like Gaius – showing hospitality to those who love the Lord.

Does not try to intimidate (vv. 9-11) – not bullying like Diotrephes.

Gospel itself is at stake (vv. 12-14) – Demetrius was genuine and full of integrity.

What we need to realise is that the whole Bible is necessary both for living and preaching, and we should not simply recycle our favourite passages time and again. This is why we have to trust the Bible to be the Bible, and not try to impose our ideas about what is relevant, but to preach what is there. But what if the passage seems to have nothing to preach and leaves us tempted to skip and go on to the next passage? Yet Paul said, 'All Scripture is God-breathed and is useful for teaching, rebuking, correcting and training in righteousness' (2 Tim. 3:16 NIV). A number of years ago, while preaching a series on 2 Samuel, there was a great temptation to miss out 2 Samuel 13, a sordid story of lust, rape, incest, murder and betrayal. But Paul did not say that 'all Scripture is profitable except for 2 Samuel 13'. I'm sure you can think of many other such passages – Genesis 38, Judges 19 and the like.

It is all too easy to skip chapters like them, or to say, 'now that Christ has come, we are not under the law.' That is a shortcut to antinomianism. More will be said of this later in the chapter on preaching Christ from the whole Bible. Nor is it enough to fit this episode into the big story, a practice which can too easily lead to saying the same thing every week with minor variations. Having fitted it into the big picture we then necd to explore the specific contribution each passage makes in its own right.

In fact, two stories are unfolding. The dysfunctionality of the chosen family reminds us of the uncomfortable truth that all families, including church ones, are dysfunctional without the grace of God. But behind this is the greater story of how God is working out His purposes. This, and other such stories, need to be read in the light of Genesis 3:15, the battle between the Serpent and the promised Redeemer. Satan seems to be riding high: lust, rape, cheating, murder and the sad inactivity of David as the judgments of 2 Samuel 12:11-12 are worked out. To take this and present it as a sermon, I suggest two main points, and a third as a kind of footnote which shows the unpleasant events in perspective.

Suggested title: **God behind the scenes.**

1. Sin perverts our humanity (vv. 1-21).
We become totally obsessed with ourselves and drown in our own feelings. Ammon has passion without love and Tamar is simply an object to satisfy his lust. Further we put ourselves in the grasp of Satan, Jonadab (v. 3) is 'Shrewd'; not the same word but the same idea of the serpent's shrewdness in Genesis 3:1. Sin creates victims (vv. 9-19). Sin disables (v. 21); David was rightly angry but did nothing. None of this is beneath us and only grace will prevent us thinking and behaving like this.

2. Sin produces hatred (vv. 22-39).
Absalom's cool and patient hatred (vv. 22ff.) is exacerbated by David's failure to enforce justice. There is an atmosphere of terror. That is the evidence of sin and death. But where is the gospel in this story? This is where the footnote is important.

3. God has provided a Saviour from sin.
If God is behind the scenes, where can we detect Him in 2 Samuel 13 and indeed in the whole cluster of stories of

which this is a part? Has David forfeited the covenant promise of 2 Samuel 7? But see 7:14-15: 'I will discipline him ...but my steadfast love will depart from him.' A little detail, easy to ignore, is that twelve times in this chapter the 'king' or 'king's sons' are mentioned. The line is secure and David's greater Son will deal with sin and death.

This is an example of dealing with a passage in its own terms and in its context, neither ignoring the bigger picture nor forcing it into every part of the text.

Increasingly, we need to explore the patterns and rhythms of the Bible and see both the part in relation to the whole and also the unique contribution of that section to the whole.

So far, in our discussion of the work of preparation we have concentrated on our study of the text, and that remains fundamental. However, if we stop there, we are in danger of giving exegetical lectures that are strong on *what?* but weak on *so what?* In a later chapter we shall look more closely at application and illustration, but here I want to say something on what John Stott called 'double listening', which is listening to the world as well as to the Word. These two listenings are not equal because the world must be judged by the Word, yet if we are to preach effectively, we need to be aware of the many other voices. 'Wisdom cries aloud in the street' (Prov. 1:20), but so does Folly and many other voices good and bad, and we need to be aware of what is being said.

When I was young, I used to worry about advice to spend half the preparation on the text and the other half on the context in the world. That, I realise, was not what was meant, but rather that the preacher's own experience, reading, other activities and interests will all feed into preaching. More will be said on this in discussing the preacher's personality, but some comments can be made here.

Effective preachers will read widely in a range of fields and such reading will differ from one to another. We need to be aware of the contemporary scene by reading books on history, politics and philosophy as well as following the news. We will all have our own interests: science, literature, the arts, music, sport and the like, and all can be grist to the preacher's mill. We also need to know our local setting well. In a congregation in a university town or in a small country village we will prepare thoroughly and preach the same message, but particularly in the area of application we will be sensitive to the needs of particular groups. The sermon is not only the outcome of the preparation in the study but of our whole lives leading up to its delivery. Walking, driving or mechanical activities provide opportunities to reflect on the message.

All of these activities from the moment we sit down at our desk until the time to deliver the sermon are only possible with the help of the Holy Spirit, otherwise we are simply going through the motions. But we must not rely on our hard work. A particular temptation for the preacher is to depend on our own diligence to the extent that we become workaholics. This is not helped when congregations expect their ministers to be available every moment of every day. After all, they work only one day a week! We need breaks and holidays and be unashamed of them. It is not that we work hard and the Spirit adds His help. Rather the fact that we are working is the sign that the Spirit is at work. A story, probably apocryphal, as many preachers' stories are, tells of a young minister who was perplexed as to whether to prepare diligently or to trust in the Spirit's help. He decided to prepare half of his sermon and leave the other half to the Spirit, and he told the congregation this was what he was doing. After two weeks, a wise lady said to him, 'It's strange that you're a better preacher than the Holy Spirit.' So, as Cromwell said, 'Trust in God and keep your powder dry.'

Chapter 5

Stimulating and sound

The need to avoid extremes
Martin Luther compared humanity to a drunk man on a horse who falls off on one side, gets back on the horse, and immediately falls off on the other. This human tendency to swing from one extreme to the other is as applicable to preaching as to anything else. Particularly, we need to avoid the tendency to be either stimulating or sound; rather we need to ensure our preaching is both. *Qoheleth* shows us a more excellent way in Ecclesiastes 12:10: "The Preacher searched to find just the right words and what he wrote was upright and true.' (NIV) 'Just the right words' is more literally 'words of delight' which appeal and give pleasure, words which are scintillating. The words are also 'upright and true'; they are sound.

Too often these are seen as opposites. 'Scintillating' is often seen as shallow; the kind of preaching which aims to entertain and cause laughter. 'Sound' is seen as heavy; undigested and unapplied lumps of theology. Undeniably, there is preaching that falls into these extremes, but that need not, indeed must not, be the case. The alternatives must not be junk food and lumpy porridge, but well-cooked and healthy meals.

It is easy to see where the two extremes come from. In some quarters, not least in Scotland, there is a suspicion of oratory which is exacerbated in the world of soundbites and Twitter. An eloquent speaker is often distrusted, and a plain bluntness is preferred. On the other hand, the desire to be entertaining and to be well thought of can take precedence over the proclamation of the truth.

How do we avoid these extremes? Let's spend a moment on the Emmaus Road. 'Were not our hearts burning within us while he talked with us on the road and opened the Scriptures to us?' (Luke 24:32 NIV) was the experience of the two disciples who had left Jerusalem disillusioned and dispirited. Notice how the risen Lord did not say, 'You don't need the Bible now you've got me.' Rather He showed them, and the rest of the church until He returns, the way in which He would be known and made known; and in verses 44-49 He shows that this witness to Himself covers the whole of what we call the Old Testament. The burning heart and open eyes are the aim of all preaching. We all have different styles and personalities (more of this in a later chapter), but we all must speak words of delight and words which are upright and true.

Now the pattern of our preaching in this as in other areas is the Bible itself and the basic structure of this book flows from the Epilogue in Ecclesiastes. Thus we will examine how the Bible portrays and presents the truth in ways which are both stimulating and sound. This is not only about rhetoric, which we will look at more fully later, but also about personality, passion and humanity. A sermon is more than a talk, but not less, and the principles of good speaking apply to preaching. We'll look first at stimulating speaking and here four things can be said.

First, stimulating preaching will show a blend of order and imagination. There must be clarity, but there must be imagination as well. I do not mean unbridled imagination, but rather presentation which both reveals clearly what the text says and also opens windows into the great vistas of truth which lie behind it. A good example of this is the Book of Ezekiel which, while full of difficult passages, has probably the clearest structure of any prophetic book. What is true of the book as a whole is also true of the individual sections within it. Let's look at its great vision of the open heaven and the glory of Yahweh (Ezek. 1).

The structure is clear: when does the vision come? (vv. 1-3); what is the vision about? (vv. 4-28a); what does the vision do? (v. 28b). The place is the land of exile (cp. John on Patmos), and the time is the prophet's thirtieth birthday when he would be mourning that he could not begin his priestly ministry; but God has a new ministry for him. So, in dismal circumstances, new vistas open up which are to be recorded in the rest of the book.

The actual vision stretches words to breaking point and is full of vivid symbolism. The cloud with flashing light is the chariot throne of God, a portable Ark of the Covenant showing that Yahweh is alive and well in Nebuchadnezzar's Babylon. His lordship of the whole earth is symbolised by the four living creatures whose wheels show their mobility in every direction under the control of the Spirit. The expanse, 'firmament' in the KJV (vv. 22-25), shows that Yahweh's authority is in heaven as well as earth. The climax of the vision is God, whose throne it is, and He wears the form of a man (vv. 26-28a). His glory blazes throughout creation.

The vision leads to awed worship, as all visions of God must. Also, a voice speaks from heaven and the prophet is not left to himself to work out what the vision means. We are not Ezekiel, but here is a great example of what true preaching is. Overwhelmed by the majesty of God, the prophet listens to the divine voice and in words of both clarity and mystery expresses something of this. Our words are not inspired like those of Scripture, but in a secondary sense, in true preaching, our imperfect words can be used by the Spirit faithfully to expound the written word and so lead us to the living Word to which the written word so fully and faithfully bears witness.

This first point about the blend of order and imagination is the basic one from which three other comments flow.

Second, preaching is a blend of the literal and metaphorical, what we might call the prose and poetry of the Bible. There are many examples: Exodus 14 is a vivid description of the crossing of the Red Sea, while Exodus 15 is a powerful poem about the God who brought about that event. But let's take what are perhaps the best examples of this: Luke 2:1-7 and Revelation 12:1-6. Luke tells with precise detail the human circumstances of the Incarnation. The words of the Emperor cause the journey to Bethlehem of a man and his heavily pregnant wife. She gives birth and her baby is born in humble circumstances. There are hints of the bigger story in the mention of David.

The same story is told in very different language in Revelation 12:1-6. Here the whole universe and the course of history is the backcloth. The woman is both Zion and Mary and the child is the One who will rule the nations. Satan is determined to destroy the child. We might call this section, 'Christmas in heaven.' Yet this is no myth, for the pregnant woman cries out in the pains of childbirth.

These passages are great for Christmas sermons, and they complement each other. 'The lowly cattle shed' is also the scene of 'the hopes and fears of all the years'. The actors in the drama are not only the humans but also the Lord Himself and the Devil as the great story beginning in Genesis 3:15 manifests itself in time and space. Also sermons on these passages are a wonderful demonstration of the unity of the Bible.

A third principle is the blend of the general and the specific. Indeed this is demonstrated in the overall pattern of the Bible itself. Beginning with the background of the whole universe the story narrows to an individual through whom all the nations will be blessed. Abraham's descendants are concentrated in a particular nation (but always with room for outsiders), and that pattern continues until all nations bless God and the Lamb in the new creation. This vision prevents both vagueness and parochialism and must be at the centre of our preaching.

Examples of this blend of the universal and local abound. Acts 8 tells of a widespread growth of the gospel as the Christians are scattered following the death of Stephen. Then, surprisingly, the Spirit takes Philip from a fruitful work and sets him down in the desert where he meets the finance minister of Ethiopia who is converted and then takes the gospel to his far-flung land, fulfilling Psalm 87:4 of people from Ethiopia or Cush becoming part of Zion. Our preaching needs to reflect this: the message is for the world but must come to individuals in particular localities (echoing what was said in Chapter 1 about knowing our world, both in its broadest sense and in its particularity).

A fourth principle is a blend of fact and imagination. In 1 Corinthians 15:1-7, Paul sets out the facts of the gospel in what is one of the earliest such statements in the New Testament. How striking and cogent these are and include circumstantial detail which emphasises the authenticity of the account. 'He was buried', a real death had happened; 'raised on the third day', an event, not the growth of resurrection faith; and the testimony of eyewitnesses. These are the unchangeable facts on which our faith depends. An old gospel hymn says, 'You ask me how I know he lives, he lives within my heart.' That's not good enough. In times of darkness I need to know that, independently of my feelings and experiences, He lives and will reign until all His enemies are under His feet. Christ has died, Christ is risen, Christ will come again.

In the rest of this chapter, with marvellous power and colour, Paul explores the implications of the facts of verses 1-8. Both the created order and history demonstrate that Resurrection is at the heart of the gospel. Life not death is the ultimate purpose of the Creator, and this fact is writ large in the created order because death, the last enemy, will be destroyed. Thus he triumphantly asserts that our labour is not 'in vain'. This is a clear link with *Qoheleth's* Epilogue because if 'under the sun' is our perspective, then our work, including the work of preaching, is certainly in vain, but we praise God who gives us the victory.

As already said, stimulating and sound are not opposites but essential companions. 'Sound' is often equated with dullness and heavy and unapplied theology. That such type of preaching does happen cannot be denied, but that it is the product of sound teaching is simply not true. It is often the product of a lack of imagination and a pedestrian literalistic style which does not warm hearts or open eyes. Soundness in teaching and living is particularly associated with healthiness as we can see from Isaiah 1 and the Pastoral Letters.

Isaiah opens his prophecy with a wealth of metaphors bemoaning the rotten state of the people. One of these metaphors is the unhealthy body and he states, 'from the sole of your feet to the top of your head there is no soundness' (Isa. 1:6 NIV). The way to put this right is to listen to the Word of God (vv. 2, 10, 18). Such listening will not only lead to right thinking but to a healthy faith.

In the Pastoral Letters, Paul develops this idea of healthy teaching, a particular concern for the Church as the apostles begin to leave the scene, and his concern is that the Church remains apostolic. In 1 Timothy 1:10 the gospel is at stake as the list of sins both of thinking and behaving in verses 9-10 shows. This provision of healthy food is particularly the responsibility of teachers and preachers and involves contending with error as well as proclaiming the truth (see Titus 2:1). Such preaching will build lives which honour the Lord and produce healthy growth both in individuals and fellowships. When we keep in mind that sound preaching is essentially healthy and lifegiving preaching, we can see how this is the other side of scintillating preaching. Three principles are important.

The first is that sound preaching neither adds to the text nor takes from it. I am not talking about the kind of preaching which refuses to accept the authority of the text but of the kind of preaching which either implies that there is not as much in the text as we want, or which avoids parts of the

Bible we don't like very much. Thus in the passage already mentioned in Acts 8 about Philp and the Ethiopian we see that there is no mention of follow up and we feel we ought to talk about it even if it's not there in the passage. We'll put it in because the Holy Spirit missed it out! This is not the same as reinforcing the message of the text by other relevant texts, which is helpful, but is introducing material into a text which is not there.

The second principle, which will help to prevent the above practice, is that we must preach the whole Bible. This cannot be done in a short time; but over the course of a ministry no part of the Bible must be left unexplored. Some parts will be covered more than others, but there is no part of Scripture which is irrelevant or unnecessary. While we need to present with clarity how to come to Christ in repentance and faith, we also need to avoid endless evangelistic addresses which advocate a particular type of conversion experience. We need to teach the Wisdom Literature, the historical books, the Prophets and the Psalms. The Pentateuch and the Gospels must feature regularly, not because they are more inspired, but because they record the great creating and saving events from which everything else flows. More will be said later about the lengths of series, but make sure no part of the Bible is neglected. Pastorally, this is vital because as book after book and genre after genre is expounded, the Spirit will reveal Christ and also the state of our own hearts. This is related to earlier comments on the importance of understanding context, and individual preachers will emphasise different aspects of the truth at different times. We will all get it wrong from time to time, but whatever we may fail to do, never neglect this priority of preaching the Word without which nothing of lasting substance will be built.

The third principle is that sound preaching will lead to desire for spiritual growth as appetites which people did not even know they had will crave for food. When people who have not encountered expository preaching hear it for the first time, often they are deeply moved in one way or another. This is to be expected for the Lord has said that His Word will not return to Him empty (Isa. 55:11). This can have a positive or a negative effect (see 2 Cor. 2:15-16). That is why we must be sure that our preaching is biblical and not simply biblically based. Preaching which is merely biblically based may start with a text, but then travel far from it and end up with sermons which are not truly biblical. The whole Bible is far more than enough for a lifetime's ministry, and you will never run out of things to say.

As we close this chapter we will look at Proverbs 9 which is a particularly good example of the combining of clarity of thought and wealth of imagination. This is the culmination of the first part of the book and along with chapters 7 and 8 gives fuller pictures of Lady Wisdom and Lady Folly whose voices have called throughout the book. The structure is plain and powerful as both women invite us to their parties which point to eternal destinies that begin in this life. Verses 1-6 describe Wisdom's party and verses 13-18 describe Folly's party. Sandwiched between them, verses 7-12 give ethical instructions. Some have argued that these verses break the sequence and are an intrusion. Rather, they give us in unmistakeable prose what the two parties are about, and the descriptions of the parties with their wealth of metaphor dramatise the eternal choices which lie behind the instructions.

Two questions arise: who gives the invitations and what ultimately are the parties? Both invitations have a superficial similarity: both call from the highest place in the city, both appeal to the simple, and both offer food. But there the similarity ends. Wisdom offers food and wine; Folly offers stolen water and bread. Wine suggests luxury and generosity (cp. Isaiah 25:6 and 55:1, as well as the wedding feast at Cana, John 2:8-10). Folly turns wine into water and her 'feast' is hasty and slapdash as opposed to the careful preparations of Wisdom.

What ultimately are the parties? Wisdom invites to a life which is one of understanding and one for which the whole of life is designed. There has been much discussion about what the seven pillars of her house are, but especially given the creation passage (8:22-30) I suggest this refers to the days of creation and the feast of the new creation. Everything has been carefully planned so that one day God's people will fully enjoy His generous provision. Folly is slapdash and her party ends in Sheol (see also 7:26-27).

These poetic passages show that verses 7-12 are not moral platitudes but powerful applications of two ways of life and two destinies. The mocker has been deluded by Folly but the wise has obeyed Wisdom's voice. The fear of the Lord, the underlying principle of the Book of Proverbs, is what gives guidance in this mortal life and hope for eternity. Ultimately all our preaching must reflect this. Preaching always calls for decision, both the initial coming to Christ and the daily obedience which marks the wise life. The poetic evocation here and elsewhere of the wise life appeals to the heart and imagination and shows that the wise life is not about rules but about relationships.

Chapter 6

Provocative and established

We have explored the necessary hard and imaginative work needed to be both sound and stimulating and the importance of engaging with the different genres of the Bible. The next area the Preacher explores in his metaphors of 'goads' and 'firmly embedded nails' refers to the overall crafting and the completed product. The emphases on sound and stimulating words and on hard and imaginative work continue in the two images used in this chapter. Preaching must be an event, but not one which is quickly forgotten, but one which carries on its work after the preacher has fallen silent.

The metaphor of 'goads' is not immediately attractive, and if we are feeling in need of a word of encouragement it may sound unhelpful. The word is usually used of prodding beasts of burden into action, with a secondary nuance, as here, of words which sting and provoke. However, as part of preaching which is to be provocative and disturb complacency, it is necessary to overcome a laziness and apathy which can so easily blight our spiritual progress.

Firmly embedded nails mean that words need to be established in people's minds and stay there. This is not static, but a continuing process. The word used for 'firmly embedded' is also used for 'planting' with the obvious implication of growth. Thus the activity is not simply a mechanical one as in fixing nails but also has nuances of the living seed of the Word which leads to growth (Isa. 55:20).

The rhetoric of preaching

The emphasis of this chapter is on what we might call the rhetoric of preaching. To avoid misunderstanding, let me clarify what I mean. The Bible is God's words and something like 90 per cent of good preaching is learning how to read it properly. Further, and this is evident in the different genres of Scripture, *how* God speaks is of enormous importance. The Lord can, of course, bless an inadequately prepared and poorly delivered sermon, but that is no excuse for not being the best that we can be. Malachi condemns the priests of his day for bringing blemished sacrifices (Mal. 1:12-14), and we must be careful to offer only our best to the Lord.

This distrust of eloquence is often justified by an appeal to 1 Corinthians 1:18-25, but we must see exactly what Paul is saying there. He is attacking the rhetoricians of the age who were far more interested in style than content and who wished to be praised for their cleverness. Paul will not have that: style must always serve substance and oratory must always serve truth. This is what Paul himself exemplifies; there are few more eloquent books than 1 Corinthians (not least the stunning fifteenth chapter). Those committed to the supreme importance of the content of the message will work hardest to strive for memorability in presentation. This chapter will look at Amos in the exploration of goads and at Revelation in examining firmly embedded nails. We shall also look a bit more at sermon structure and its important place in the overall message.

The significance of Amos

Amos' book preserves a sample of his preaching sometime in the reigns of Uzziah of Judah (791-740 B.C.) and Jeroboam II of Israel (793-755 B.C.). The exile of Israel to Assyria, which is a main subject of the book, happened in 722 B.C. It probably was delivered over a brief period 'two years before the earthquake' (Amos 1:1). This short book abounds in vivid observation, oratory, vision and penetrating comment. Amos exposes the complacency and shallowness of Israel's life with clarity and compassion and has much to teach us, not least in his rhetorical devices and powerful use of language.

The use of paradox

Amos is a master of paradox and uses this device to confront us with different sides of reality. In particular he presents massive truths about God which goad us out of complacency and see truths we would often rather not see. 'The LORD roars' is the opening picture; Israel's God is not a tame lion. The 'roar' here is the terrifying pouncing roar of the lion as it launches itself on its prey. Often we would rather have a cosy Santa Claus figure who makes no demands and simply wants us all to have a good time. But how could a 'god' like that have created heaven and earth or be the Lord of history? Of course, He is tender and slow to anger, but unless we tremble with fear we will never appreciate His grace. Grace is only good news when we realise that we deserve judgment.

That paradox is spelled out further in the rest of chapters 1 and 2. Judgment is pronounced on Israel's neighbours such as Edom and Moab and we can imagine Amos' original hearers feeling smug and superior. Yet the Lion's roar comes to Judah and Israel, who are even more guilty because they were rescued from Egypt and given the Torah and knew what pleased Yahweh. In case they had missed the point Amos shows the paradox of being in covenant with the Lord and yet behaving as if no such covenant existed. The Lord's words in 3:1-2 strike at the heart of complacency. Being chosen is not an excuse to live in any way we like but will lead to more severe punishment if the relationship is broken.

'Chosen' (2a) in the NIV is more accurately 'known' and is a covenant word used in Genesis 4:1 of the intimate relationship of Adam and Eve. The word 'punish' is more accurately 'visit', a word used in Genesis 50:24-25 as the dying Joseph assures his family that God will surely 'visit' them and take them back to the promised land (a promise repeated in Exodus 13:9). Here the word is turned on its head, not that God will reverse His covenant, but that the bitterness of exile will produce a chastened remnant who will return.

This is developed further in 9:7 where the lordship of Yahweh and His care for all nations is emphasised. Yes, God brought the Israelites from Egypt, but He also brought the Philistines from Caphtor and the Aramaeans from Kir. This is not a denial of the covenant but a warning not to treat it as a badge of superiority. Such a realisation will affect our preaching by making us humble and lead to emphasising grace and judgment as two twin and not contradictory truths. So preach the paradoxes of the Bible: providence and free will; goodness and severity; the incarnate God; the meeting of love and justice at the cross, and the like.

Provocative language

Amos is also provocative and uses vivid, sometimes violent, language to make his point. 'Hear this word, you cows of Bashan,' is perhaps not as rude in Hebrew as in English, but it is hardly a compliment! Do not see this as anti-women; see the attack on wimpish men in 6:1-7. We all tend to glamorise sin, especially our own favourite sins. The truth about sin is that it is not glamorous; it is ugly and petty and offensive. We must not take the references to fine food and wine (6:4-6) as an attack on the blessings this world often affords, but as warnings not to trust and be dependent on things 'under the sun', and this emphasis needs to be reflected in our preaching. Unsurprisingly, Amos has a lot to say about worship because sincere worship and effective preaching belong together. This is especially the case in chapter 5 where the blend of lament (5:1-17) and denunciation (5:18-27) is a mark of true preaching. Judgment must not be preached as if we are gloating, but must be tempered by a real empathy with those to whom we are preaching. This is exemplified elsewhere in Scripture particularly by Moses (Exod. 32:30-32) and Paul (Rom. 9:3), who both were willing to accept damnation if their people could be saved. Neither could save their people, but there was One who could, and at the end of strong denunciations of the teachers of the law (Matt. 23:1-36), our Lord Jesus Christ mourns over the very people who had rejected Him (Matt. 23:37-39). Amos gives us robust theology with vivid language, and we must strive to do the same.

Action and stability

'Goads' and 'nails' are a good balance, with the one speaking of urgent action and change of attitude and the other of firmly fixing in mind and heart. It is interesting that while 'firmly embedded' has the obvious meaning of stability, the verb also has the secondary meaning of plant (e.g. Psalm 80:5), and thus the nuance of growth. We shall examine this metaphor particularly by looking at the Book of Revelation which is not only the end of the New Testament but the culmination of the whole canon.

The Book of Revelation

One of the fascinating features of the Book of Revelation is that while there are hardly any direct quotations from the Old Testament, every verse, almost every phrase, echoes the earlier Scriptures. We shall look first at the 'bookends' of the Bible, Genesis 1 and 2 and Revelation 21 and 22, to see how their joint message firmly embeds the message of the beginning, and which has significant developments that carry on the story. Among other things, this book brings together the theology of the Bible and orientates it to the future so that we can live faithfully in the present.

The bookends of the Bible

The whole of God's plan is encapsulated in these four chapters from creation to new creation. Our preaching needs to teach the big picture of the Bible, not necessarily by giving overviews, although they have their uses, but by placing each book in the unfolding pattern while showing the book's distinctive contribution. 'Big picture' preaching, if we are not careful, will end up saying the same thing every week. As we study the imagery of creation and new creation in these 'bookend' chapters, we see continuity, such as the river and the tree of life. This is Eden restored, but more than that. Yahweh is no longer a visitor but lives with His people (Rev. 21). The tree of life is now on both sides of the river, symbolising super abundant life. This is the tree which heals (Rev. 22:3-5). And leads to fuller life. The ancient Serpent can no longer destroy (Rev. 20:1). But look especially at the last verse (Rev. 22:21). This has been from Genesis onwards a story of grace, and grace has won the victory. God and His people are home forever without need of ceremonies and rituals: 'I saw no temple in the city' (Rev. 21:22). This does not contradict Ezekiel 40–48 which sees a new temple; rather both passages draw attention to the same reality of God's presence but from different angles.

Universal and particular

The whole Book of Revelation continues to unfold the course of salvation history emphasising both the broad sweep and specific times and places. The title, 'Letters to the Seven Churches,' is somewhat of a misnomer as the whole book is a letter to the churches (1:9-11). Each needed a word for their specific situation in Roman Asia towards the end of the first century; but each needed to hear that in the wider context of not just the other churches but in the overall purposes of God in goodness and severity. Revelation 2 and 3 are not a potted history of the Church from the first century onwards. These are real communities in their towns, but they also represent the whole Church across time and space with the besetting temptations and the divine help. The ultimate reality of the Throne of God is presented in chapters 4 and 5, a throne that governs what happens in both heaven and earth, and helps us to live in the present. The judgments of God are not so much a continuous sequence of events as parallel accounts of God's judgments *in* history before the final judgment *on* history. The Judge is the Lamb who was slain and has the authority to open the scroll of history (5:6-10), an authority coming from His sacrificial death as well as from His power over creation.

The importance of structure

A feature of sermons which powerfully expound those amazing truths is a strong structure. The so-called 'rule of three' is not a rigid pattern to be used exclusively, but at its best it helps people to remember and appreciate the point of what you are saying. You need not call it 'three points', but three acts in a play, three circles spreading out as you skim a stone across the water, and the like. It is important that your headings are not simply descriptive, but that they analyse and begin to apply what you have discovered in the text. Many years ago I heard a powerful sermon on John the Baptist from Luke 3 by the New Testament scholar, Professor Kingsley Barret. He said that the Baptist preached in the wrong place, to the wrong people, and indeed preached the wrong message. These headings brilliantly unfolded the paradoxes of the Gospel with its bypassing of sacred buildings, religious hierarchy, and the leading figures of the time. The headings were deliberately designed to be memorable and provocative.[1] Sometimes headings will flow. More often, there will be hard work in finding them, but if we are committed to unfolding the Word with clarity and power, we will not grudge the time spent.

At other times the structure of the passage may suggest a different approach, such as in Psalm 46. The heart of the Psalm is verses 4-7 about the presence of God in His city, symbolised by the river which is plainly the river of Paradise. From that vantage point, the psalmist looks out at God in the created order with its storms (vv. 1-6) and in history with its battles (vv. 8-11). Thus we could have:

God is with us (v. 7).

Even when creation is threatening (vv. 1-6).

Even when warring nations encircle us (vv. 8-11).

---

1. See the helpful comments by J. A. Motyer on analysis and headings in *Preaching?*, (Christian Focus Publications, 2013), pp. 89-99.

Big truths about God – even supreme on His throne He cares for His people. The use of Jacob emphasises our weakness and unworthiness. The assurance that God is with us enables the psalmist and us to look at the raging waters of creation and history with a faith that does not ignore the enemies, but which shows their power is subject to the Creator. At the heart of Israel's faith was the assertion, 'my help comes from the LORD, the Maker of heaven and earth' (Ps. 121:2 NIV). Thus nothing in heaven and earth can thwart His purposes (see Romans 8:39). Also the use of Jacob is significant: as we read his story, and find his waywardness and selfishness lurking in our own hearts, we are again shown that we owe everything to grace.

Worship in heaven and on earth
But returning to Revelation and its encapsulation of the Bible's plot line we can see the same pattern across the book working out in history as well as the created order. The worship of heaven in chapters 4 and 5 is both a present and future reality (see Hebrews 12:22-24). When God's people gather on earth, even in small numbers, they join with angels and archangels and all the company of heaven. Remember that when you are preaching to thinly attended gatherings. What is happening is of eternal significance and the buds on earth will one day flourish into the full blooms of heaven. The imagery of the rainbow round the throne takes us back to Noah and to Ezekiel's vision of the chariot throne of God who was present in Nebuchadnezzar's Babylon. 'Seeing him who is invisible' is how Hebrews 11:27 describes Moses' persevering faith, and having something of that kind of faith is necessary as we preach heavenly realities. The worship of heaven focusses on the big truths of creation and redemption, another reminder of the need to preach on great subjects and their relevance to earthly as well as heavenly life.

Now in the light of then

The worship of heaven sets the scene for the Lamb's opening of the scroll and the subsequent judgments of the seals, bowls and trumpets which are to culminate in the final judgment. God's people do not escape these judgments, but they are protected through them and assured of final victory; both notes need to be sounded in our preaching. As I have suggested, these successive judgments are not so much chronological as parallel and, for example, the trumpets (8:6–9:21) have many echoes of the Plagues of Egypt, which shows again the consistency of God's ways. The Exodus is the great saving event of the Old Testament and points to Calvary where Christ our Passover Lamb was sacrificed for us. The whole Bible is the gospel, and we shall explore that further in the chapter on preaching Christ. Revelation is the culmination of Scripture, not a strange book tagged on at the end. I know it has often been used to advance bizarre speculations, and more interest has often been shown in compiling the sequence of events which will lead to the End rather than demonstrating its practical relevance about living now in the light of then. Preach Revelation and some will look up and continue on their journey with greater vigour and renewed hope.

As always, substance and style go together and words which provoke and remain fixed doing their work are part of applying Scripture. Good structure will open eyes and begin to apply the message in a way which will be remembered. These examples from Amos and Revelation could be multiplied across Scripture and are inspiration to us as we work at our sermons.

Chapter 7

All that we need

A characteristic of God is His overflowing generosity. This is expressed in 2 Peter 1:3: 'His divine power has given us everything we need for life and godliness' (ESV). Much of the rest of the letter is concerned with the gift of the Scriptures, the words of the apostles and prophets which will firmly establish us and cause us to see clearly. These 'very great and precious promises' (1:4 NIV) show how important a deepening knowledge of the Bible is as we live our lives in this world.

The Preacher warns of addition to the words 'given by the one Shepherd'. We shall explore Preaching Christ in a later chapter, but here our concern is with the authority of Scripture of which its sufficiency is an important part and how that relates to our preaching.

The Westminster Confession of Faith sets out this doctrine clearly as part of its long first chapter 'Of the Holy Scripture: The whole counsel of God, concerning all things necessary for his own glory, man's salvation, faith, and life, is either expressly set down in Scripture, or by good and necessary consequence may be deduced by Scripture: unto which nothing at any time is to be added, whether by new revelations of the Spirit, or traditions of men' (1.V1).

It is worth taking a little time to reflect on what this does and does not mean. First, it means that only in Scripture do we find God's words and thus they both embody and limit the subject of our preaching. Does this mean we should not preach through, for example, the Nicene Creed? That kind of preaching would be useful if we make sure our exposition emphasises the words of Scripture which underlie the statements of the Creed and that the Creed's validity and usefulness depend on its faithfulness to these words.

Also, far from running out of things to say if we stick to Scripture, we will soon find that there is more than enough to occupy us for our entire ministries. Our predecessors often preached series of mindboggling length. William Still, commenting on Martyn Lloyd Jones' thirteen years on Romans and fifteen years on Ephesians said, 'the Lord would have needed to give him a ministry of 500 years to cover the whole of Scripture in such depth.' Even such marathons are short in comparison with forty years or so, which we have heard of. If you are a young preacher, don't ever be afraid that you will run out of material even if you preach much shorter series! What you will be continuing to do is try to give a balanced diet: short letter followed by extensive narrative; Gospel and Old Testament wisdom, and the like. The best way to do this is by the exposition of books, although all of us will, from time to time, do seasonal or topical expositions. We will allow no such thing as a 'no go' area in Scripture and we will emphasise the need of a whole Bible for all we need in life and godliness.

The authority and sufficiency of Scripture means that our total view of reality will be governed by Scripture and that we will avoid pointless speculation. We will be continually mindful of avoiding the way of legalism (which is the gospel with additions, where it is not enough to be saved by grace through faith, but various practices which characterise the lifestyles of various groups have to be added). We will also avoid the way of liberalism (which is the gospel without the great supernatural lifegiving truths, and the Christian life becomes little more than bland moralistic platitudes). What both of these ways have in common is that Christ is not enough. In the way of legalism He can only save if works are added; in the way of liberalism He is not the biblical Lord, the conqueror of sin and death and the One who will reign until He has put all His enemies beneath His feet (1 Cor. 15:25).

In our preaching we need to avoid unwarranted speculation, not least in the areas of creation and eschatology. That does not mean that we should avoid them, but it does mean responsible treatment which sees how the pattern develops throughout Scripture. Indeed the more a doctrine such as the Return of Christ has been made the subject of extravagant theories, it has been the more necessary to preach it in its biblical balance and fullness. This applies more widely, not least to preaching biblical truth about godly living.

A good chapter to illustrate this is Matthew 23 which is about meeting Christ in judgment. The chapter is a sober one for preachers because it is addressed to those whose theology is impeccably orthodox, who 'sit in Moses' seat' (v. 2 NIV). They wear clothes which symbolise authority and they love the outward trappings of power. We need to be very careful how we interpret this. There are godly men who wear clerical robes and who preach the gospel with power and clarity. We cannot judge people's hearts, but generally speaking where such matters are emphasised they can easily become dominating. C. S. Lewis, speaking of the Lord's Supper, said that if we believe a truly supernatural event is happening, the less important it becomes where the celebrant stands or what he is wearing. The same applies to preaching. We must not slip into the opposite extreme of a self-conscious informality which also draws inappropriate attention to an individual.

The preacher further needs to be truly human with a heart which beats with true humanity. These teachers (23:23) certainly observed the letter of the law in precise detail. That was not wrong, but they had no similar concern for 'justice, mercy and faithfulness'. All of us struggle with desire for prominence and the need to be faithful. The pulpit is a dangerous place and human pride a continual temptation.

But what of preaching on the great cataclysmic moments which punctuate God's activity in history and His revelation to humans? We will use as an illustration for this, Matthew 24 (see also Mark 13 and Luke 21), often known as the 'Olivet Discourse' or the 'Little Apocalypse' which has been the subject of great controversy. Were these sayings delivered as a single discourse or were they a selection of utterances from different times placed together? The first seems more likely as each has its own coherence, and search for sources easily distracts from the main purpose. What I am interested in here is preaching the Second Coming and neither omitting important truths nor surrendering to unbridled speculation. I was brought up in 'Premillennial Tribulation Circles' where a distinctive view of Christ's return had developed. It argued that the Return would be in two parts, drawing very heavily on 1 Thessalonians 4:13-18 which speaks of the *Parousia* or Rapture. This was seen as a 'secret' event when the Lord would return to take His people to heaven. Then would unfold the Great Tribulation, at the close of which the Lord would return visibly and in great glory; this event was called the *Epiphany* or Manifestation, after which would follow the Millennium (variously understood), and then the 'Eternal State' would follow (this was based on a particular interpretation of Revelation 20). This view was popularised by John Nelson Darby, one of the leading teachers among the Brethren, and was given classic form by the notes in the Scofield Bible. I recognise this account is somewhat simplified, but I do not want to detract from the main subject of this book but instead appeal for a biblical approach to this important subject.

Two comments must suffice at this moment. The first is that godly people, including my own parents lived and died in this belief; we must respect the views of those who sincerely love the Lord and want to follow His Word.

The other is that, nevertheless, I believe the view is profoundly mistaken. There is no hint in Scripture of a two-stage return. The idea that a 'secret event' would be heralded by the Lord's cry of command, the archangel's voice and the trumpet of God, is hard to believe. Also the view in its classic form draws a distinction between Old and New Testament believers which cannot be sustained.

I think that digression was necessary before looking at what do we preach from Matthew 24 and other passages about the Return. Like all prophecy, it has both near and distant fulfilments. The events first describe the destruction of Jerusalem by the Romans in A.D. 70 (more specifically referred to in Luke 21:20-24). But that event prefigures the greater event of the Coming which is still future to us as it was to them. There are numerous different interpretations of the Discourse, some of which emphasise one or another horizon. What I want to do here is take this as an example of a passage we might preach on the Coming without over speculation but highlighting the important features present in different proportions in all passages dealing with this subject.

Three important emphases are present. First, the Coming will be a cosmic event (vv. 29-31). Just as the star the Wise Men saw (Matt. 2:2) showed that the child born was not only the king of the Jews but the king of heaven (language reflecting Numbers 24:17), so here the cosmic disturbances show God shaking up His creation. The renewing of the universe is an inseparable part of God's plan to reconcile all things to Himself. This is developed in Romans 8:18-27 where the 'glorious freedom of the children of God' is an integral part of the removing of the curse from creation. Once humanity has become like Christ and is able fully to resume the ancient mandate to rule the earth, then the created order will rejoice in its freedom.

Second, the Coming will bring judgment (vv. 31-41). As the Flood brought both judgment and salvation, so will the Coming. It will come into the ordinary events of life, and the elect will be gathered into the Lord's immediate presence.

Third, and a necessary implication of the second emphasis, the Coming has a practical effect on our lives (vv. 42-50). Live now in the light of then is at the heart of the message. The parables which follow in chapter 25 deal with different aspects of patient watching. Watching is not simply passive; there are duties and responsibilities to be carried out and these will be rewarded in the end. Indeed far from creating an attitude of otherworldliness, the more certain we are that the Lord will return to wind up the affairs of this world and usher in a better one, the more urgent it is that we engage in all lawful and worthy activities until He comes.

These three emphases are present in all passages looking to the Coming. It's important to add a comment on the language and imagery used. The great saving events all hang together as God works to fulfil His ancient purpose. When we mention one, the others are implied. Thus Matthew 24:31 alludes to Daniel 7:13-14. But in that chapter 'one like a son of man' approaches the throne of 'the Ancient of Days', which refers to the Ascension rather than the Coming. To see that as contradictory is to miss the point. The Ascension (often a neglected doctrine) is proof that Calvary was acceptable to God and that in the power of resurrection Christ ascended to receive the kingdom which will grow until His Coming. A similar point can be made about Revelation 1:7 where the words are applied to the Coming. Then in the remarkable imagery of Revelation 12:1-6, the apostle sweeps straight from Incarnation to Ascension, encompassing the drama of redemption in a few vivid words. Preach the Coming and show its centrality.

The Shepherd

The Preacher has already introduced us to the 'one Shepherd' (Eccles. 12:11), the source of his own authority, and in our next chapter we will explore what it means to preach Christ. However, a few words about the Shepherd metaphor would be appropriate here.

The Shepherd is Yahweh Himself (see Psalms 23 and 80), but under-shepherds are an important part of His providential care. This is powerfully expressed in Psalm 77:20: 'You led your people like a flock by the hand of Moses and Aaron.' The most significant human shepherd is David: 'He chose David his servant and took him from the sheepfolds; from following the nursing ewes he brought him to shepherd Jacob his people, Israel his inheritance. With upright heart he shepherded them and guided them with his skilful hand' (Ps. 78:70-72).

We must not sentimentalise the metaphor; of course there is gentleness, but there is also power and strength. This is well illustrated in Isaiah 40. Tenderness is beautifully expressed: 'He will tend his flock like a shepherd: he will gather the lambs in his arms; he will carry them in his bosom, and gently lead those that are with young' (Isa. 40:11). But who is this tender Shepherd? He is the Lord God who 'comes with might and his arm rules for him' (Isa. 40:10). This is the Sovereign who is reversing the exile and destroying the Babylonian empire, just as in Psalm 77 He brought about the Exodus. In the New Testament, the Lord Jesus Christ is the Shepherd, and we will explore this further in the next chapter.

Chapter 8

The Word must become flesh

We noticed in Chapter 1 the danger of exalting preachers into gurus and called for the importance of preaching rather than preachers. That does not mean that the preacher's personality is unimportant. Just as the Word becomes flesh uniquely and fully in the Lord Jesus Christ, so the Word must be incarnated in the preacher. This is vividly illustrated when Ezekiel was told to take the scroll and eat it (Ezek. 2:9–3:3). John had a similar experience (Rev. 10:10). The message comes through a human personality. We shall look first at what to avoid and then at some positives.

What to avoid
One thing to avoid is trying to imitate a favourite preacher. There is nothing wrong with admiring a preacher and indeed learning more about the mystery of preaching through him. However, what we learn must be from what he says and not from an attempt to be like him. Learn about good exegesis, clear structure, vivid language, and the like. But each of us is a unique individual and the truth must come through our individual personality.

Another danger is of a stilted and over formal manner. In earlier times, preachers were often said to speak in an excessively solemn manner in what was sometimes called the 'holy whine'. This, at least in my experience, is less common today. There is a right kind of seriousness, and this is not a plea for flippancy but for using the whole range of our personality. Humour is legitimate as a means of catching attention and often showing the absurdity of certain types of behaviour. In avoiding an over solemn manner, it is important not to go to the opposite extreme of an unstructured and banal informality. Again that fails to use the whole range of personality.

Most serious of all is being unconvinced of the life-changing power of the Word, of refusing to allow the Bible to be the Bible. This will convey to the listeners that we do not really believe what we are saying. If we are not changed by the message we bring, no one else will be. If that is the case, one of two things is likely to happen. The first is that we will continue to speak words which are true but with decreasing power and conviction. The other is that we will cease to value preaching and concentrate on other things.

Positive matters

But let's turn to positives. The first thing to say is obviously that we all have different personalities. Not only that, but from region to region and country to country, personality is expressed in different ways. Given that what we are looking for is authenticity, this surely comes from honesty in the preacher who is true to the text and expounds it in a way that is true to himself. Let's explore that a little.

There must be a growing familiarity with the Bible and not just the passage we are preaching on. We need to read our Bible so that we will know Christ better (see previous chapter). Such reading, incidentally, will continually give us ideas for sermons and sermon series. It will help us to grasp both the big picture and the contribution of specific passages within it. Most importantly it will lead to a growing love for and knowledge of the Lord.

In case what was said earlier is misunderstood, learn from good preachers not to imitate but to be inspired. The internet has given us increasing access to preaching resources and we need to use these wisely and with discrimination. Read earlier sermons as well, always separating the eternal truth from what belongs to their era.

That is related to what we might call living in the real world. We need to know the communities we serve, the nation and the world. This was something we touched on in Chapter 1. We all have our own interests and emphases, but in the providence of God He has given each of us experiences which are valuable in our preaching. I am very glad my early studies were in English literature which was a great training in how to read texts. Then I taught English for a number of years, trying to convey that fascination to teenagers. Others will have different life and professional experience which will have fed into their preaching practice.

Believe in the Holy Spirit without whom no preaching will ever be effective. This may seem passive, but it has important practical implications. This means that our study as well as the act of preaching must be guided by Him. Ultimately it is not our knowledge of ancient languages, our familiarity with commentaries, or even our homiletic skills which make us preachers, although all these are valuable; it is the presence of the Spirit in the study as well as the pulpit. Do you ever sit at your desk with a blank piece of paper or computer screen in front of you? That is a time to pray for divine help and illumination. Have you been deeply moved in the study, perhaps weeping or laughing? If we are not moved in the study it is unlikely that we or anyone else will be stirred in church. The more we believe in the power of the Spirit the more we will plan and prepare according to our capacities and abilities. Praying must be part of our preparation.

Be honest with and about yourself and know your strengths and weaknesses. If your sermons are recorded, force yourself to listen to them because that will at least partially help you to see yourself as others see you and often helps to identify and remove irritating mannerisms. If you have trusted friends who comment because they love and care for you, so much the better. We all have the voices we were given, but we need to train ourselves to use these to the full as well as to learn the value of the significant pause and other rhetorical devices.

Care deeply about the people to whom you are preaching. This is especially essential if you have a regular ministry with a particular congregation and have an increasing knowledge of their joys and sorrows and the circumstances of their daily lives. However, many of us are itinerant preachers and not familiar with congregations we visit. We must remember that the Spirit is totally familiar with them, and we need to pray that what we say comes home to their situations.

There needs to be passion in our preaching. That will differ from person to person and place to place. It does not mean shouting or thumping the book board, but the fire which comes from the Word itself. Jeremiah speaks of this: 'there is in my heart as it were a burning fire' (Jer. 20:9); and in his prophecy he uses all the resources both of prose and poetry to convey that. The good news must be announced with feeling, although sometimes it can sound as if someone was announcing train times or the like. This is not a worked-up and artificial passion, but the overflow of a heart touched by the Spirit and anxious to share the good news with others. I mentioned Whitefield in Chapter 1, and many commented on his extraordinary preaching.

Realise that we have to fight the powers of darkness. This is true of every Christian, but the devil has a particular hatred of Christ being proclaimed. We must not become obsessed with Satan, nor must we ignore him. Make Ephesians 6:10-20 part of you; there Paul is particularly concerned that the gospel is proclaimed boldly. The devil is 'the father of lies' and needs to be resisted with the Truth, the one weapon he cannot stand against.

We need to keep on being 'transformed by the renewing of our mind' (Rom. 12:2). Not, notice, by the renewing of our emotions. We have already seen the importance of emotion, but our feelings are fickle, and we need to have clear thinking and not depend on our passing moods. When we preach, we need to appeal to minds as well as to hearts, and thus to wills where alone radical change will happen. Transforming of the mind is related to wide and discriminating reading and interest in big ideas. It is also linked to close and careful study and meditation. Meditation is not emptying our minds but opening them to great truths.

We need to cultivate a spirit of praise. This is not a false optimism or ignoring of temperament. Nor is it a call to be continually upbeat and laughing. Read the Lament Psalms. Rather it flows from a conviction that the Lord is in charge and working out His purpose. The bleakest of the Laments, Psalm 88, ends in darkness but never denies that the Lord is 'God of my salvation', the words with which it opens. The psalmist, like Job, never lets go of that ultimate truth that the Lord's purposes are saving ones. This is not whistling in the dark, but a holding on to the Lord in the conviction that He is holding on to us. Our sermons must ultimately be doxologies.

We need to build up resources. It's important to have a good library of commentaries. That does not necessarily mean a huge number. As *Qoheleth* points out, not everything written is valuable. We need to discriminate, not least because commentaries tend to be expensive. In Chapter 2 we looked at some of the commentary series available and here I simply want to make a few comments on the use and misuse of commentaries.

It is important we have some heavyweight commentaries which will give us relevant background, written by people who know the biblical languages and history to help us avoid building on shaky foundations. These will seldom give preaching hints, but they will help us get into the book. If we are preaching, for example, on 1 and 2 Kings, we need to know about Assyria and Babylon and how they brought about the exile. A Bible atlas is also valuable in the understanding of many books, not least the Gospels. But we must not overload our sermons with historical and geographical information.

We will also have commentaries which are concerned with expounding and applying the text, and, as suggested in Chapter 2, we will use these after our main preparation is done. Other theological works are needed to sharpen our perception and open our eyes to new vistas of truth, and we will do well to read at least some of the great spiritual classics such as Augustine's *Confessions* and Calvin's *Institutes*.

Self-discipline is important. There will be discouragement as well as blessing, and both are part of the ways in which the Lord develops our characters. We need to know our limitations and realise that we cannot convert people or cause them to grow. When blessing comes, we need to remember that it is God alone who brings it. We need to stick at it and believe in our calling. There will be right times to move from particular situations, usually signalled by other openings, and we need to be sensitive to such times.

God uses all types of personalities
Perhaps most important of all, God can use any type of personality. The key is certainty that we have been called to the task. Just as there are different types of personality so there are different types of call; compare Isaiah 6 and Jeremiah 1. Isaiah 6 is an overwhelming experience: the majesty of the Sovereign seated on His throne, the seraphim or 'burning ones', the earthquake and the smoke recalling Sinai. In Jeremiah 1 the Lord uses the humble almond branch and the domestic image of a boiling pot, but the call is no less real. Indeed both are warned of opposition and rejection, and both carry out their ministry for over forty years.

So it is today with diverse personalities and diverse calls. Some are extroverts and perhaps in danger of over flamboyance. Some are introverts and timid. The Lord can use both, and other personality types, provided they are humble and teachable.

Personality matters, but it is not the thing that matters most. *Qoheleth* tells us to 'Cast your bread upon the waters, for you will find it after many days' (Eccles. 11:1). Our responsibility is to sow; we do not know when the seed will fall by the wayside and when it will produce a hundredfold. A seventeenth-century English merchant was on an extended trip to Scotland, and he took advantage of hearing some of the notable preachers of the day. First, at Irvine he heard David Dickson and 'he showed me all my heart'. Then he visited St Andrews and heard Robert Blair who 'showed me the majesty of God'. Also in St Andrews he heard 'a little fair man called Rutherford' and he 'showed me the loveliness of Christ'. Very different personalities, doubtless very different styles, but all preaching great truths at the heart of the gospel.[1]

So, whatever our personalities, let us keep casting our bread upon the waters, and do it continually as we 'do not know which will prosper' (Eccles. 11:6). It is doubtful if any of these preachers knew of the words of the merchant, and there will be many times when we are totally ignorant of the effect of our preaching. So let's keep on sowing and leave the results to the Lord of the harvest.

---

1. The story is told by Rev. Robert Wodrow, minister of Eastwood, near Glasgow, in the early eighteenth century, a historian particularly of the Covenanting era, in his work *History of the Sufferings of the Church of Scotland from the Restoration to the Revolution.*

Chapter 9

Truly human preaching

As *Qoheleth* comes to the end of his book, he sums up his message by making great assertions about God and humanity which control the way we live and think and thus control our preaching. This is 'the end of the matter' for which the rest of the book has prepared. 'Fear God and keep his commandments for this is the whole duty of man' is how the ESV renders 12:13b, and most of the translations have a similar rendering. But there is no word for 'duty' in the Hebrew text. This is not an obligation laid on humanity but a statement of what it means to be human.

What does it mean to be truly human?
All of us would agree that we need to be truly human in our preaching to speak authentically to human beings. When it comes to preaching, many colleges and courses assume that the way to do that is to give pride of place to the human sciences such as anthropology, sociology and psychology, often at the expense of biblical languages being sidelined into uncongenial hours such as 4pm on Fridays. These studies have their value, but they do not touch the heart of the matter. Only as we know God can we bring to humans a life-changing

message. In this chapter we will look at fear and obedience and how these shape our preaching.

What is the fear of God?

This is an idea we are sometimes inclined to water down for fear of offending people and thus we try to say it means something other and lesser than fear. Often too it is related to a narrow idea of relevance. The Bible is relevant, and we do not need to make it so. However, often we see relevance as related to people's felt needs, which of course matter, but concentrating on those can make preaching simply sound at best as good advice and at worst as nagging, neither of which will produce transformed living. Whereas preaching which concentrates on the living God will lead to a sense of awe, mystery, trembling and sinfulness which lead to radical change. After all, 'God is in heaven and you are on earth' (Eccles.5:2). We must not think of God as simply a greater and more powerful version of ourselves.

The word 'fear' here and its related noun occurs over 400 times in the Old Testament, and there are other words in both Testaments which have the same emphasis. Even when the word is not used, the idea is regularly present: think of Isaiah 6, Psalm 96 and Revelation 1. Nor is it confined to theophanic passages. Think of Luke 5:8 where Jesus causes a miraculous catch of fish and Peter falls at His feet saying, 'Depart from me, for I am a sinful man, O Lord.' But let us examine some biblical uses of the word.

Some biblical occurrences of the word

As mentioned, there are many hundreds of references, but a few examples will show its significance. In Genesis 3:10, Adam says, 'I was afraid because I was naked, and I hid myself.' Consciousness of sin and the fear of God belong together. Then in Exodus 3:6, 'Moses hid his face, for he was afraid to look at God.' There the overwhelming holiness of God expressed in fire causes fear as at Sinai (Deut. 5:5). A particularly rich example occurs in 1 Samuel 12:24 where Samuel says to the people, 'Only fear the LORD and serve him faithfully with all your heart. For consider what great things he has done for you.' The mighty acts of God are a powerful incentive to fear Him. 'To God be the glory, great things he has done.'

The Ecclesiastes reference in chapter 12 is characteristic of the Wisdom Books. 'The fear of the LORD is the beginning of knowledge' (Prov. 1:7) sets the tone for Wisdom. It is important to realise that 'beginning' is not an elementary stage that we leave behind but rather the controlling principle of the whole of life. An illustration might help. Shakespeare's work depended on using the alphabet he had learned as a child. However rich and powerful his use of words, he never ceased to build on that knowledge. Thus the fear of the Lord is not only for when we first become conscious of His holiness and our sin but something which must continue to shape us.

Some implications of the fear of God

One important implication of the fear of God is that it will save us from other fears, many of which the Preacher has mentioned. There is the underlying fear that everything is futile and transitory and the ultimate fear of death itself. As preachers it is so easy to fear people's opinions and assessments more than fearing God. 'Fear Him, you saints, and you will then have nothing else to fear.' This will help us to look to the only 'well done' which ultimately matters.

The fear of God will also profoundly affect our worship. **There are no rules**, but worship must have a sense of awe and expectancy as we bring our offerings of ourselves into the presence of His holiness and open our hearts to His life. Paul's use of the interesting phrase, 'the church of the living God' (1 Tim. 3:15), gives us a clue. He does not say 'the living church of God' for that would place the emphasis on the people; rather he shows that any life a church may have comes from God alone and not from our liveliness.

But the fear of God is not simply for the gathered church, it affects our everyday lives. As George Herbert says, 'A servant with this clause makes drudgery divine: who sweeps a room as for thy laws, makes that and th' action fine.'[1] That can be applied to the routine business of preparing to preach as well as the actual moment of delivery.

We need to have big ideas of God and teach these right from the beginning. When small children sing, 'My God is so big, so strong and so mighty, there's nothing that he cannot do,' important truths are being sown in their young minds which can grow and develop later. Because God 'has put eternity in man's heart' (Eccles. 3:11), nothing less can ultimately satisfy us, and nothing less than a God-centred ministry will reach the unconverted and build up Christians.

But we must turn now to the second phrase which relates to God's commandments.

Keeping His commandments

At first sight this seems straightforward enough, but there have been continual disputes as people have swung between legalism and antinomianism. It clearly cannot be legalistic to obey God's commands, but problems arise if these are mixed with men's commands and if they are presented in a censorious and moralistic way. The Preacher has already pointed out the danger of self-righteously rejecting God's gifts: e.g. 'Go eat your bread with joy, and drink your wine with a merry heart, For God has already approved what you do' (Eccles. 9:7). Don't feel guilty as you enjoy a romantic candlelit dinner and 'enjoy life with the wife whom you love' (Eccl. 9:9). Let's explore obeying God's commands a little more.

Obedience is about relationships

A hugely important statement is made by Jesus to His disciples just before He goes to His death. 'If anyone loves me, he will keep my word' (John 14:23). Obedience is a product of love. Not we *should* do this and that, but as God's children we are called to show the family likeness. That will transform our

---

1. From his poem 'The Elixir'.

attitude to difficult commands. 'Take his easy yoke and wear it, love will make obedience sweet.'[2]

Obedience is a matter of the heart

While the commands of God obviously cover things to do and not to do, the emphasis is much more on basic attitudes, matters of the heart which govern what we do. What we are, and even more what we are becoming, is at the heart of obedience. This is a constant theme in the Wisdom Books as well as in the Sermon on the Mount and the ethical sections of the New Testament letters. This is made plain early in Proverbs: 'Keep your heart with all vigilance, for from it flow the springs of life' (Prov. 4:23). Wise living, discreet speaking, avoiding evil and pursuing good, all flow from that. Similarly, the Sermon on the Mount begins with attitudes which govern behaviour in the Beatitudes (Matt. 5:2-11). We can never in this earthly life obey the Lord perfectly, but we can increasingly obey Him acceptably. The heart is the key because the heart is the basic person. Unless we preach from the heart, other people's hearts will not burn within them as they did on the Emmaus road.

Obedience is the key to holiness: 'having purified your souls by obedience to the truth' (1 Pet. 1:22). It is, as Peter also says, 'being born again, not of perishable seed but of imperishable, through the living and abiding word of God' (1 Pet. 1:23). Obedience is thus a living transformation by the Word of God which the Spirit applies to our hearts so that we may share it with others. Peter continues to show how this will lead to integrity, to battling the powers of evil, to positive relationships in the community, and within marriage.

This is all very far from rules and regulations and has much more to do with a growing and deepening relationship with the Lord. The right way to live is the obedient and reverent life which is the product of fearing God. Fearing and obeying belong together and must not be separated. Two passages will give us further material to reflect on.

---

2. From the hymn 'Come you souls, by sin afflicted'. Joseph Swain (1761-1796).

Isaiah 66:1-2 brings together the overwhelming greatness of God and the frailty of humans but in such a way that the very majesty of God becomes the ground of human hope. Isaiah is full of majestic celebrations of the awesome nature of the Lord springing from the prophet's experience in chapter 6. God is the supreme Lord of creation and history (see chapter 40), and here at the end of the book that sovereignty will be revealed more fully in the new creation. He cannot be confined in human structures because He fills heaven and earth. Yet this does not lead to contempt for humanity but rather to an opportunity to know Him. Two elements are vital. The first is humility and sorrow for sin which will remove the pride which prevents us fearing and obeying. The other is trembling at God's Word.

How will that trembling show itself particularly in a preacher? First, it will mean we will never sit in judgment on God's Word. We talked earlier about allowing the Bible to be the Bible, to set the agenda and ask the questions. Particularly when the text seems puzzling and uncongenial, we must realise that the limitation is in ourselves not in God's Word. It will mean we must never use parts of the Bible to set aside other parts, especially those which speak of judgment (more of this in the next chapter). Isaiah realises that this will sometimes lead to criticism by those who do not tremble. 'Hear the word of the LORD, you who tremble at his word: "your brothers who hate you and cast you out for my name's sake have said, 'Let the LORD be glorified that we may see your joy,' but it is they who shall be put to shame"' (Isa. 66:5). This is another case where the fear of God will deliver us from the fear of humans.

It will also mean never shirking preparation and working hard to gain a deeper understanding. It means that as preachers we must take the Bible with total seriousness but not take ourselves too seriously. Isaiah sees that we cannot tremble before the Lord without trembling before His Word. Jesus makes the same point: 'whoever is ashamed of me and of my words in this adulterous and sinful generation, of him will the Son of Man also be ashamed when he comes in the glory of his Father with the holy angels' (Mark 8:38). The Word must be proclaimed fully and fearlessly.

In Revelation 1:9-17,the apostle John, exiled to Patmos, has an overwhelming vision of the risen Lord and he 'fell at his feet as though dead' (Rev. 1:17). But this true fear is dispelled as the Lord lays His hand on His servant and says, 'Fear not.' Surely a classic example of the Lord's words speaking right into the point of need. This experience is to be passed on for all those who would come after. John further shows his trembling at the Word he had received, warning at the end of the book neither to add or to subtract from it (Rev. 22:18-19), a warning which applies by extension to the whole Bible.

It is fascinating to see how this passage shows the difference between the fear of God and the fear of man. The Lord is not telling John to have no fear or trembling of His revelation in glory, rather He is reminding him that this will relativise other fears. The emperor (probably Domitian) is able to put people in prison or on Patmos, and put them to death, but there his power stops. The living One who died and is now alive for ever holds the power of the world to come where the emperor's writ does not run. The message that John is given is not only for his own time but for all time, and indeed all eternity where all creation bows to the Lamb on the throne. That is the message passed on to us as well and we are called to persevere, knowing that the Lamb holds the scroll of history.

Ultimately when we fear and believe God we are saying that the gospel comes to us from outside and, as Paul says, it was not received from any man but through a revelation of Jesus Christ (Gal. 1:11-12). This means we have no authority to alter it to suit the contemporary culture and thus rob it of its power.

Some lines from a poem make an important point:

For me 'twas not the truth you taught,
To you so clear, to me still dim.

But when you came to me you brought
A sense of Him.[3]

Here are vital truths about preaching. We need not expect everyone to understand everything at first hearing. Rather, when there are open hearts the Spirit can work before there is clear understanding of what is said. Just as He takes our inarticulate prayers and presents them to the Father (Rom. 8:26-27), so He can take the imperfectly understood Word and work at a deep level until it is understood more fully. That is why there is no place for dumbing down and being simplistic; the Spirit who breathed the Word uses it to convict and convert.

Above all, the preacher comes from God's presence, bringing something of the Lord and thus speaking to people's deepest needs and longings. 'A sense of Him' – that is what preaching is ultimately about and that can never be boring.

---

3.   From the poem 'Indwelt' by A. S. Wilson.

Chapter 10

When the chief Shepherd appears

The Preacher has one more thing to say and it brings Ecclesiastes to a satisfying conclusion. Verse 14 of chapter 12 is not, as some commentators argue, a pious addition but an answer to the deep longings expressed in the book: 'For God will bring every deed into judgment, with every secret thing, whether good or evil.' The point is that everything is ultimately not vain and ephemeral. Judgment is frightening and can only be faced in fear and obedience, and yet it is also encouraging because it means that everything has eternal significance. For those called to be under-shepherds who pass on the words of the one Shepherd, this has particular emphasis. That is why I have chosen as the title of this chapter the words of Peter, 'When the chief Shepherd appears' (1 Pet. 5:4). Not only is life not meaningless, neither is preaching meaningless, and it will be assessed by a higher court. Thus judgment to come is part of our living and thus part of our preaching.

How we regard preaching
We saw in Chapter 1 how important it is to see preaching as an event, and this is reinforced here. We never know how long we have left; each sermon could be the last. This is not

being morbid, but it is 'numbering our days, that we may get a heart of wisdom' (Ps. 90:12). This is well expressed in the words of Richard Baxter: *I preach as never sure to preach again, And as a dying man to dying men.* The issues of life and death and eternity need to be real in our thinking and thus become real to others.

Preaching and Wisdom
We have looked at the Wisdom Books previously as well as emphasising the Preacher's Epilogue, and it would be useful to look again at how preaching on Wisdom is important for a sense of eternity. If our horizons are limited to 'under the sun', while it is true that 'wisdom excels folly' (Eccles. 2:13 NKJV), there 'is no wisdom in Sheol' (Eccles. 9:10). But in the eternal world, where God will bring everything into judgment, wise choices and right living matter. This is the particular emphasis of the extended treatment of wisdom and folly in Proverbs 1–9. Right from the beginning it is emphasised that choosing wisdom is never merely an intellectual exercise, although the mind is important. Rather it is a call to a relationship. 'I stretched out my hand' (Prov. 1:24) says Wisdom and describes a life change which avoids Folly. Folly, like Wisdom, is personified as a woman (2:16), in her case a 'forbidden woman', and the contrast continues throughout the subsequent chapters until in chapter 9 both women invite us to their parties.

In Proverbs 7, Folly, with vivid imagery, creates the ambience of seduction and flattery (vv. 10-18) and thus makes it easy for the gullible young man to be ensnared. There is a contrast between the naivety of the young man, who probably thinks he is being clever and daring, and the reality, which is that 'he does not know it will cost him his life' (v. 23). That this is more than an unfortunate mistake, but has eternal consequences, is shown by his final destination not being an exotic and enticing bedroom, but Sheol (v. 27).

Chapter 8 builds up a picture of Lady Wisdom and her place in creation. She calls to a lifestyle which is godly and in tune with the created order. Instead of Sheol, the wise who

96

listen to her find life and divine favour (v. 35). Her words have no perversity or intent to deceive.

In chapter 9, both Wisdom and Folly issue party invitations and at first sight they look alike. But the menus are different: Wisdom offers wine and rich food and Folly offers stale bread and water. As noticed in a previous chapter in this book, the structure of this chapter in Proverbs is important. Wisdom's invitation is 9:1-6 and Folly's is in 9:13-18. In between, 9:7-12 give a series of ethical instructions which seem out of place, but are in fact an integral part of the chapter. They tell us that these invitations are not simply to a party but are about life choices and the destinies which flow from these. The party imagery shows that total personalities and experiences are involved. The party (as in Isaiah 25 and the parables of the kingdom) is a picture of the new creation with its abundance and blessing. As we preach on eternal realities we must show the wonder of the world to come, and the blessings God has prepared.

Facing reality

The poet T. S. Eliot said, 'Humankind cannot bear very much reality.'[1] The task of truly biblical preaching is to open people's eyes to the reality of judgment which is part of the doctrine of God. One of the ways in which Jesus opened eyes to reality was by parables. We will look at one of them here, that of the rich man and Lazarus (Luke 16:19-31). We shall not attempt a full exposition, doubtless many will have preached on this passage, but examine some points which particularly relate to judgment and preaching.

As in Proverbs, choices made in this life have consequences in eternity; not that the rich go to hell and the poor to heaven, but that both narrative and dialogue dramatise eternal realities. We have to remember the situation in the first century, a world without social services or poverty relief, and thus the only help the destitute could hope for was if the rich took care of them, which is why Lazarus was placed at this rich man's gate.

---

1. In his poem 'The Four Quartets'.

He was seriously rich; gate implies a gated compound, and the dogs would be guard dogs. Lazarus was totally destitute; he was unable to walk ('laid' implies he had to be carried). He was so poor that scraps from the rich man's table would have satisfied him. Yet he is the man who is named. The rich man is nameless. I know some call this the parable of 'Dives and Lazarus', but this is a misunderstanding of the Latin text which says there was a man who was *dives*, which means rich. This nameless man is totally selfish and that remains true of him in eternity as the dialogue shows (vv. 24-31).

The rich man still regards Lazarus as a mere errand boy; twice he says 'send Lazarus' as if the social distinctions on earth still applied. The rich man shows no remorse or repentance and has failed even in Hades to appreciate reality. He is still the centre of his world. Lazarus, by contrast, is next to Abraham, the man of faith *par excellence*.

The other striking feature of this story is the importance of Scripture: 'they have Moses and the prophets.' That is the Word we have, and we have it more fully as we now have the complete canon. It is important to remember that the gospel word is not something accompanied by the power of God but is itself the power of God. The Lord in His providence may choose to work miracles, but it is the living Word which leads to the living Lord and that is why we need to preach it with all our hearts.

Personal impact

The story is vivid and unforgettable, but it would be all too easy to distance ourselves from it by thinking, 'Well, I'm neither like the rich man nor Lazarus.' So let's look at 1 Corinthians 4:5 where Paul says, 'Do not pronounce judgment before the time, before the Lord comes, who will bring to light the things that are hidden in darkness and will disclose the purposes of the heart. Then each one will receive his commendation from God.' This is close to Ecclesiastes 12:4; indeed Paul may be echoing it, for he knew the Scriptures so well that even when he was not directly quoting he was often alluding to texts.

The context is about the right way to regard the servants of Christ which is part of Paul's own conflict with the Corinthians and their attitude to ministry. Verse 1 has a fine balance: Paul and other faithful ministers are 'servants of Christ' which shows humility and dependence. But they are also 'stewards of the mysteries of God', the plan of salvation now fully revealed in Christ, which speaks of privilege and responsibility for faithful and reliable communication. The only judgment which matters is the final one, so the assessments of others and even self-assessment is limited and partial. This means that no human will pronounce final judgment on our preaching. Realising that will save us from pride when plaudits come and from despair when criticisms multiply.

None of this should lead to complacency from preachers; not all criticisms are wrong, but the passage is a spur to faithfulness. The emphasis here is positive, 'receive his commendation from God.' Not that everything will be done and said perfectly in preaching, but that sincerity and faithfulness will be honoured. Hidden things, both here and in Ecclesiastes, will include the process of preparation which only the Lord sees and knows about.

Some principles of judgment

Looking to the final day must become part of our spiritual landscape and experience and not just something tagged on at the end. Judgment has begun already. Even before we all 'appear before the judgment seat of Christ' (2 Cor. 5:10) we aim to please Him every day of our lives. Appearing at the judgment seat does not mean that we will lose our salvation; our sin has already been dealt with when we came in repentance and faith to Christ. It does mean that we live in the light of eternity as we fear God and keep His commands.

Final judgment does not mean that we don't keep on reviewing our practice and strive to improve. As preachers we never 'make it' and we must remain students to the end of our days. Learn from early efforts and listen to good advice and follow good models without slavish imitation.

Who is sufficient for these things?
These words of Paul in 2 Corinthians 2:16 are part of his impassioned defence of his ministry to his detractors in Corinth who argued that real authority and true preaching were marked by success and glamour and not by suffering and frequent rejection. In face of this argument, the apostle introduces the surprising metaphor of the triumphal procession. This is not about Paul's personality but concerns his gospel ministry and its dealing with the issues of life and death which are bound up with people's responses to Christ. Some will smell the stench of death and reject the living Word who comes in the written word. Others will smell the fragrance of Christ and turn to Him in faith. We are not Paul, but we have Paul's God and Paul's gospel, and it is vital to reflect on his words here in our own circumstances because we are certainly not in our own strength sufficient for these things.

Three points can be made. The first is that 'our sufficiency is from God' (2 Cor. 3:5). The message does not come from us, but it is the Spirit of life Himself who takes words on a page and uses them to bring life and hope. Such words will be written 'on tablets of human hearts' (2 Cor. 3:3) says Paul, echoing Jeremiah 31. Our words can educate, inspire, entertain, provoke, but without the Spirit no one will be converted or grow in grace. It's important to realise that we cannot in the true sense of the word preach at all without the Spirit and we need to believe that not just as a theory but in our hearts.

Second, this is not saying 'let go and let God' as if we had no part to play at all. Paul says in 2 Corinthians 2:17 that we are not to be 'peddlers of God's word' but 'men of sincerity'. He speaks later of the 'super-apostles' (2 Cor. 11:5) who valued success and appearances, seeing the gospel as a commodity which if presented attractively enough will be sold. Yet our hard work and our diligence in prayer matter, not as a substitute for the Spirit, but as ways in which the Spirit works. Use all the resources available and always aim at becoming better heralds of the gospel.

Sincerity must be at the heart of all our living and working. In terms of preaching it means total submission to the Scriptures and never misrepresenting them especially when we find what they say uncongenial. It means not cutting corners and watering down the impact of the Word. It involves 'the open statement of the truth' (2 Cor. 4:2). Above all it means what 'we proclaim is not ourselves, but Jesus Christ as Lord' (2 Cor. 4:5). I remember a church where on the lectern were the words, 'Sir, we want to see Jesus,' a powerful reminder that as preachers we are not there to present ourselves and our ideas but to be channels of the aroma of Christ. The phrase 'aroma of Christ' is a fascinating one and probably originally recalls God smelling the sacrifices with pleasure. But more generally it speaks of the beauty of Christ who comes in the Word; you may remember how Samuel Rutherford's preaching 'showed the loveliness of Christ', a recurrent theme in Rutherford's preaching and writing.

Third, just as our living is 'in Christ', so must our preaching be. Indeed 'Offer Christ to them' were the words John Wesley spoke as he commissioned preachers. No one who has read thus far will take that to mean endless evangelistic talks but rather full biblical exposition which sees Christ as the destination to whom all paths in Scripture lead. There will be instruction, courses, and surveys of the whole biblical landscape over the course of a ministry, but the rich variety will have a unifying heart as we expound in the Scriptures the Lord Himself. We close with a prayer which I have found especially helpful before preaching as it brings together our weakness and God's power.

Father, I pray that as we come to your holy Word, you will take my human words in all their weakness and imperfection; that you will use them faithfully to expound the written word and so lead us to the living Word, the Lord Christ Himself in whose name we pray. Amen

Also available from Christian Focus Publications...

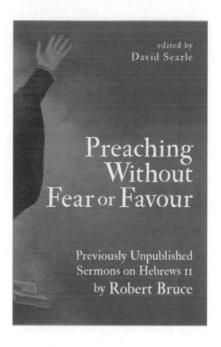

edited by
David Searle

Preaching
Without
Fear or Favour

Previously Unpublished
Sermons on Hebrews 11
by Robert Bruce

ISBN 978-1 52710 363 4

Preaching Without Fear or Favour: Previously
Unpublished Sermons on Hebrews 11

by Robert Bruce

Born into a noble Scottish family in the sixteenth century,
Robert Bruce turned his back on earthly prestige and wealth
to enter the ministry. He was Minister of Edinburgh for twelve
years, preaching to the King and the court. These sermons on
Hebrews 11 show a truly remarkable example of post–reformation
preaching, heard in the Great Kirk of St Giles, in the heart of
Scotland's capital. David Searle has undertaken the huge task of
putting these sermons into the English alphabet, translating them
from the Braid Scots, so they can edify the church today.

Christian Focus Publications

Our mission statement –

STAYING FAITHFUL

In dependence upon God we seek to impact the world through literature faithful to His infallible Word, the Bible. Our aim is to ensure that the Lord Jesus Christ is presented as the only hope to obtain forgiveness of sin, live a useful life and look forward to heaven with Him.

Our books are published in four imprints:

CHRISTIAN FOCUS

Popular works including biographies, commentaries, basic doctrine and Christian living.

CHRISTIAN HERITAGE

Books representing some of the best material from the rich heritage of the church.

MENTOR

Books written at a level suitable for Bible College and seminary students, pastors, and other serious readers. The imprint includes commentaries, doctrinal studies, examination of current issues and church history.

CF4·K

Children's books for quality Bible teaching and for all age groups: Sunday school curriculum, puzzle and activity books; personal and family devotional titles, biographies and inspirational stories – because you are never too young to know Jesus!

Christian Focus Publications Ltd,
Geanies House, Fearn, Ross-shire,
IV20 1TW, Scotland, United Kingdom.
www.christianfocus.com